THIS BOOK HAS BEEN DONATED TO EVERY SECONDARY SCHOOL LIBRARY IN AMERICA. IT IS A TREASURED GIFT THAT SUPPORTS THE OBJECTIVES OF THE CONGRESSIONAL MEDAL OF HONOR SOCIETY TO INSPIRE AND STIMULATE OUR YOUTH TO BECOME WORTHY CITIZENS OF OUR COUNTRY.

★ ★ ★

We would like to acknowledge and thank the following organizations for their participation in this noble endeavor. Without their support this project would have never come to fruition.

THE CONGRESSIONAL MEDAL OF HONOR SOCIETY

"As recipients of the Congressional Medal of Honor we sincerely hope that what we have shared herein demonstrates to you what is meaningful about life. Through our comments and stories it is the courage to make the right choice, commitment, drive, loyalty, honor, integrity, honesty, love, and selflessness that is important in being a successful and worthy American."

THE CASTLE ROCK FOUNDATION

"Of the thousands of societies and special-interest organizations in America, the Congressional Medal of Honor Society has to be the most prestigious and its members the most honored. These men are our nation's heroes. The individual deeds of these heroes are an integral part of American history and should be known to all our young people as they study history. It is a pleasure and an honor for the Castle Rock Foundation to provide the means that puts this volume in your library."

FULCRUM PUBLISHING

"These are the stories that exemplify the American spirit—solid examples of leadership and selflessness in the face of adversity. At a time when our nation needs heroes, it is extremely gratifying to be able to place this book in the hands of our young people."

MILITARY ORDER OF THE PURPLE HEART — CHAPTER 423

"Our membership believes it is important to the youth of our nation to understand the sacrifice that veterans have made to preserve the heritage and freedom of this great country. This book provides an insight into those sacrifices: all gave some, some gave all."

$\mathcal{B}$eyond *the* $\mathcal{M}$edal

A Journey
from Their Hearts to Yours

Peter C. Lemon

John May these stories make you proud to be American!

Fulcrum Publishing
Golden, Colorado

In Memory of Contributors Now Deceased

John Bulkeley
Jesse Drowley
Joseph McCarthy
Charlie Morris
Dirk Vlug

Copyright © 1997 Peter C. Lemon

Book design by Jay Staten
Photographs for the cover, back and flap by
Don Jones Photography, Colorado Springs, CO
Interior photographs were generously provided by the
Congressional Medal of Honor recipients or their families.

Library of Congress Cataloging-in-Publication Data
Lemon, Peter C.
   Beyond the Medal : a journey from their hearts to yours / Peter C. Lemon.
        p.   cm.
   Includes bibliographical references.
   ISBN 1-55591-358-X (hardcover)
   1. Medal of Honor. 2. United States—Armed Forces—Biography. 3. United States—Biography.
I. Title.
UB433.L46 1997
355.1'342—dc21   96–47641
                                                                           CIP

Printed in the United States of America

0 9 8 7 6 5

Fulcrum Publishing
16100 Table Mountain Parkway, Suite 300
Golden, Colorado 80403-1672
(800) 992-2908 • (303) 277-1623
www.fulcrum-books.com

*This work is dedicated to those comrades
closest to us at the time of battle
for which we received the Medal of Honor.
We are indebted to you, for without your support
and, in many cases, your life,
we certainly would not be here today.*

*The Medal is as much yours as ours.
We are honored that you would allow us
to hold this distinction on your behalf.*

Thank You

The generation that carried on the war has been set aside by its experience. Through our great good fortune, in our youth our hearts were touched with fire. It was given to us to learn at the outset that life is a profound and passionate thing. While we are permitted to scorn nothing but indifference, and do not pretend to undervalue the worldly rewards of ambition, we have seen with our own eyes, beyond and above the gold fields, the snowy heights of honor, and it is for us to bare the report to those who come after us.

—Oliver Wendell Holmes
United States Supreme Court Justice, 1884

Contents

The Congressional Medal of Honor

"For Conspicuous Gallantry and Intrepidity in Action
At the Risk of Life
Above and Beyond the Call of Duty"

They're our "Knights of the Round Table." So revered is this award that President Harry S. Truman once said, "I would rather have the blue band of the Medal of Honor around my neck than to be President." So remarkable are the acts of heroism that earned them the Medal that countless movies and books have attempted to capture the glory throughout modern history.

The Medal of Honor is our nation's highest military award that can be bestowed upon a service member.

Those who have been granted the privilege of wearing the Medal come from—and have returned to—all walks of life. From rural America and the inner cities, we know no ethnic boundaries. We are laborers, farmers, politicians, military members, schoolteachers, business owners; and yes, some of us have even spent time in jail. Despite this diversity, our personal lives have a common thread, and that tie that binds is our unwavering devotion to our country in the name of freedom.

Along with the acclaim and prestige, the Medal of Honor also brings with it great responsibility to all recipients. The recipients are often asked to speak at schools, to participate in parades, to be interviewed by the press, to provide mentoring for children—the list goes on.

The recipients are under a public obligation that is accompanied by an intense national scrutiny. They are almost obligated by the distinction to uphold a higher standard of purpose and resolve than others—sometimes beyond what is humanly capable. We muse that F. Scott Fitzgerald was wrong when he claimed, "There are no second acts in Americans' lives." He must have overlooked the Medal of Honor holders when he penned that. We strive to fulfill our country's expectations in peace as we did in war.

Established by a Joint Resolution of Congress on July 12, 1862, during the Civil War, the Medal of Honor was this country's first military award for valor in action against an enemy of the United States. The award is recommended and awarded by the military but is presented by a high official (usually the president of the United States) in the name of the Congress of the United States. This is why it is referred to as the Congressional Medal of Honor.

There are currently three Medals of Honor—one for the United States Army, one for the United States Air Force and one that is presented to the United States Navy, United States Marine Corps and United States Coast Guard members. The army has the largest number of recipients, while the Coast Guard has but one.

The medal itself is an inverted, five-pointed star (with different distinctive center markings for each military service) and hangs from a light blue silk ribbon. It is the only American military decoration that is worn around the neck; all others are pinned onto the uniform.

The criteria for this award are stringent, requiring a minimum of two eyewitnesses to the action, with the person having voluntarily performed the deed *at risk of his own life*. The action must also be one that outstandingly displays *conspicuous gallantry and intrepidity, above and beyond the call of duty*.

The first Medals of Honor were awarded to six soldiers upon their release from a Confederate prison. The Medals were presented March 25, 1863, for their actions in April of 1862 during "The Great Locomotive Chase," when the soldiers stole the locomotive *General* in Big Shanty, Georgia, some two hundred miles behind enemy lines and drove it ninety miles north, destroying bridges and rail lines along the way.

The most recent action for which the Medal was awarded was in the battle at Mogadishu, Somalia, in October of 1993. Randall Shughart and Gary Gordon, two members of the U.S. Army's unique Ranger Delta Force, selflessly volunteered to go to the aid of a downed helicopter crew who lay wounded and about to be overrun by the enemy. The two gallantly protected the crew until they were killed themselves.

The Medal has been presented 3,452 times to 3,433 recipients, which sounds contradictory but is correct; there are nineteen men who were double recipients of this award.

Approximately six out of every ten medals are presented posthumously. This brings us to the sobering realization that the majority of the recipients sacrificed their lives during the action that earned them the award.

Of the roughly 35,300,000 that served in World War I, World War II and the Korean and Vietnam Conflicts, only 954 servicemen received this distinction; 540 posthumously. This puts into perspective the rarity of the selfless action for which they received the award.

Twenty years have passed since any living person in the armed forces of the United States has performed an action for which the Medal was awarded. The living recipients continue to pray that no one will ever receive this award again—a sure sign that we are one step closer to world peace.

There are 154 living Medal of Honor recipients, with more than one hundred of those being World War II veterans, most of them well advanced in years, the eldest being ninety-two. As a group, they are becoming extinct; the membership is reduced with each month that passes.

To form a bond of brotherhood among all living recipients of the Medal of Honor, the Congress of the United States chartered the Congressional Medal of Honor Society on August 14, 1958. All recipients are invited to membership. It was organized for charitable and educational purposes to foster patriotism, promote allegiance to our government and its principles and to inspire our youth to become worthy citizens of our country.

As we leave this world, we ask that the stories of our deeds and lives live on. We ask that you remember not only those who have received the Medal of Honor, but all the civilian and military members who have served this great country of ours, the United States of America.

Acknowledgments

I am extremely grateful to the following people for their contribution to this book. Without their support, this miracle would have never happened.

To Jim Waller who was with me from the beginning, spending countless hours editing, finalizing the entire manuscript, finding more of my mistakes than I care to admit, but redlining the manuscript so I would laugh. I'm blessed that you walked into my life. And to his family, who supported his late-night behavior to accomplish this project in such a short period of time.

To Christine Manning for encapsulating the initial citations, and to her four young sons who had to give up time with Mom so she could complete this work. Thank you for being sensitive.

To my dear friend, Alan "Rapp" Rappaport, who was always there for me twenty-six years ago, as he is now. Your wealth of information and insight is truly appreciated. I love ya buddy!

To Reverend Rebecca Dunlap for providing spiritual guidance and being a friend when I needed it most.

To the author of *Country Classics* and my dear friend, Ginger Mitchel, who kick-started me when I had no idea where to begin. We sure had some great laughs.

To Van, Faye, Dave, Linda, Randy, Lou, Tammy, Fern, Jeff, Anne, Frank, Dick, Carol and all my friends who continue to believe in me. Thank you for your love and acceptance.

To the Congressional Medal of Honor Society staff, especially Mike Williams and Beverly Vanvalkenburg for whom I am indebted for fulfilling my numerous requests.

To all the wonderful staff at Fulcrum Publishing, notably Bob Baron, Jay, Dianne, Patty, Alison, Sam and Carol. It's terrific to be part of such a remarkable team.

To all the Congressional Medal of Honor recipients and their families who were willing to share themselves with the world, thank you. You have my profound admiration.

To my children, I love you! Thank you Laura and Luke for asking the right question and always loving and supporting me even when I became grouchy at the computer. Nate, thank you so much for assisting with the initial cover design.

Introduction

The book you are holding in your hands is meant to be the answer to a question posed to me last year by my two children—Laura and Luke, who were then ages eleven and nine.

We were returning from the Congressional Medal of Honor Society Biennial Convention, which had been held in Philadelphia. My children had accompanied me to many of these functions during their short lives, but for some unknown reason, this trip was different. Maybe it was seeing the Liberty Bell and the site of our first Continental Congress, or maybe they were at "that" age—I still don't know what prompted the question. What I do know is that I was taken by surprise and therefore had no ready answer when they said:

"Dad, we've been to lots of these things before, and we know what the Medal of Honor is. We know they all have the Medal—but who *are* they?"

That was inspiration enough. If after all these years and the many events, my children still didn't know who the people were behind the Medal—and were curious enough to ask—then how much more obscure must they seem to the public at large?

It would be my responsibility, as one of the youngest living recipients, to capture the essence of these individuals and to share their personal stories with the world. This volume is the result of that one innocent question from my children.

Never before has anyone attempted to capture the essence of these individuals, the real flesh-and-blood person, beyond the Medal.

As each living Congressional Medal of Honor recipient was contacted, their offerings arrived in fits and starts. So, this work did not come together in true anthology fashion, but instead like a child playing with a bag of marbles, peeking inside to find wonderful patterns, natural and uncontrived. Nor were their responses staged by interviews. Each selection is a personal and natural offering.

As adults, we often feel obligated to start at the beginning of a book and read right through to the end. But in this, I urge you to "look in," to "read around," just as you will. Open its pages here and there, reading whenever and wherever you choose. Isn't that how life is?

The recipients' wonderful words on patriotism, personal struggles, spirituality and family values will touch your heart, tickle your funny bone, feed your soul, press a tear from your eye or be a beacon of inspiration. You'll get a glimpse of these heroes on a very personal level—a compilation of their innermost thoughts, insights and wisdom.

Accompanying each personal vignette, or story, is a companion piece. A capsule, illustrating the spirit of the recipient's valiant deed, drawn from the official military citation that describes the date and action for which they received the Congressional Medal of Honor. A bibliography is provided in this book to encourage you to read the official military version of each heroic act.

I'm conscious of the fact that by reading this book we're making history together. We have met at a crossroads in life's journey that takes us beyond the Medal. I trust that the Medal of Honor will now become animate through your becoming intimate with the recipients. After you have read this book and met the recipients of the Medal of Honor, I trust you will number us among your friends.

This book is such that I hope you feel free to dip into the bag, to "take a peek." If one special marble catches your fancy, it's yours to take with you on your life's journey.

Please enjoy *Beyond the Medal*. It is indeed a journey from a special place in their—our—hearts to yours.

—Peter C. Lemon
Medal of Honor Recipient
Echo Company RECON
2d/8th Cavalry, 1st Cavalry Division

Beyond *the* Medal

... over ice-covered barren ground, with absolutely no protection, Wiedorfer alone voluntarily charged two gun emplacements and miraculously silenced both with rifle fire and grenades. Minutes later he assumed command of the platoon after its leaders were wounded ... .

Private Paul J. Wiedorfer, U.S. Army
Company G, 318th Infantry, 80th Infantry Division
December 25, 1944
Near Chaumont, Belgium

No Better Price to Pay

The Congressional Medal of Honor—
it certainly altered my life in many ways
from 1944 to the present day.

The older I get the more I think how wonderful it would be
if there were no longer a single living holder
of the Medal of Honor in the United States of America.

That would mean that we finally learned how to live in peace.

There could be no better price to pay for the elimination of the Medal of Honor
than a truly peaceful U.S.A.
and a truly peaceful world.

I wonder if we will ever learn.

I pray to God that we do.

Paul Wiedorfer

... despite his own wounds, under constant intense enemy fire, Taylor valiantly and repeatedly entered burning and exploding armored vehicles to rescue a total of fifteen comrades wounded when his armored cavalry troop was ambushed just west of Que Son.

First Lieutenant James Allen Taylor, U.S. Army
Troop B, 1st Cavalry, Americal Division
November 9, 1967
Near Que Son, Vietnam

Challenge a Challenge!

I remember once when I was seven or eight years old, my father and I were sitting in a duck blind on the banks of Humboldt Bay near Arcata, California. I was cold and miserable, but I hid my feelings; I wanted to prove to my dad that I was a "duck hunter." Little did I know that what I was about to experience would forever affect my life.

A small flock of green-winged teal circled our decoys and began their descent amongst them. "Let's take them, son," Dad shouted, and we both stood up and began shooting. Dad dropped three birds—I missed. Grinning, he put his hand on my shoulder and asked, "Why are you looking like that? What did you do wrong?" Disappointed, I responded, "Why ask me something like that!"

His answer has helped me to meet and overcome many challenges.

> *"Son, you will encounter many high and low points*
> *throughout your lifetime and hundreds of obstacles.*
> *But don't be afraid to make or admit a mistake.*
> *Turn a negative into a positive, challenge a challenge,*
> *and never say you can't do something.*
> *Think about what you have done, right or wrong,*
> *improve or correct it, and move on to the next challenge.*
> *Through positive thinking, hard work, dedication and*
> *sacrifice you can succeed."*

Allen Issac Taylor, born November 1903, died in May 1962,
I love and miss him.

Jim Taylor

... as an unarmed medic, alone and completely exposed to the enemy, Doss single-handedly carried seventy-five wounded men to a cliff's edge and lowered them by rope to safety. He then retrieved a wounded man two hundred yards beyond the battle line, enduring fire and grenades, and within eight yards of the enemy, made four trips to drag the wounded to safety. Although wounded himself, Doss returned another comrade one hundred yards to safety through enemy fire ... .

Private First Class Desmond T. Doss, U.S. Army
Medical Detachment, 307th Infantry, 77th Infantry Division
April 29–May 21, 1945
Near Urasoe-Mura, Okinawa

Miracle Day

I was brought up in a Seventh-Day Adventist home. Our beliefs are shown in the name: We keep the seventh day as the Sabbath as given in the Fourth Commandment of God's Ten Commandments, and we believe that Jesus is coming back to earth soon to take His people to heaven. I still believe this with all my heart.

My mother faithfully took my older sister, younger brother and me to Sabbath school and church each Sabbath day and saw to it that we received a Christian education in our church school.

An experience I had at this time had a great influence on my attitude. When I was in the first grade, they didn't hire a janitor to clean the school, pupils cleaned the schoolroom. My job this one day was dusting the erasers. I discovered that by rubbing them together they would look clean without my having to knock them together to get the chalk dust out. My wise teacher came to the blackboard, picked up the erasers and banged them together—the chalk dust flew! She said, "Desmond, a job that isn't done right isn't worth doing at all." I never forgot that and have used it for my motto all through my life.

That teacher later went to China as a missionary. I admired her, and it made me want to be a missionary, too. I did do a little missionary work when I was in the Pacific—at Uncle Sam's expense.

Shortly after my parents were married, my dad bought a picture at an auction sale of the Ten Commandments and the Lord's Prayer illustrated. It now hangs on my living room wall. The illustration for the Sixth Commandment, "Thou Shalt Not Kill," was of Cain killing his brother Abel.

I looked at that picture hundreds of times and wondered, "How could a brother do such a thing?" It gave me a horror of killing that influenced my actions when I was in the army.

When I was drafted into the army in 1942, I asked for a noncombatant classification, but the draft board officer said there was no such classification, and I would have to go in as a conscientious objector. He explained that if I went in under any other classification I could be court-martialed if I refused to do ordinary work on my Sabbath or refused to bear arms.

That was the background of my life before I went to the Pacific in 1944. I served in Guam, Leyte and Okinawa. I would like to relate one story that happened on Okinawa.

This happened the day before I lowered approximately seventy-five injured men down the face of the Maeda Escarpment to safety, for which I received the Medal of Honor. This is an experience I like to call the "Miracle Day."

We had been fighting for the escarpment, where the cliff was about four hundred feet high. The top thirty-five feet of the cliff formed an overhang, jutting out five feet or so over the thirty-five feet immediately below, so we had to put up a cargo net to storm the top. We had been fighting for four days. The Japanese were dug in on top of the hill in caves and hollow places that looked like natural terrain, so it was hard to fight them.

On the morning of "Miracle Day," we were to go up on the escarpment again. I mentioned to Lieutenant Gornto that I believed prayer was the greatest lifesaver there was, and I thought the men should pray before they went up on the escarpment. He quickly called the men together and said, "Doss wants to pray." Now that wasn't what I had in mind—I meant each man should pray himself.

But I did pray that the Lord would help the lieutenant give the right orders as our lives were in his hands, and that we would all use safety precautions, and that each man would make his peace with God before he went up the cargo net.

With that we went up and almost immediately got pinned down. Company A was fighting on our left, and they were badly shot up so we were ordered to take the whole escarpment by ourselves. We started forward and knocked out eight or nine Japanese underground positions. The amazing, miraculous thing was that no one in our company was killed, and only one man was injured—by a rock that hit his hand.

It was such an outstanding happening that our headquarters heard about it and sent the Signal Corps up to investigate. How would you like to hear the report that went back to headquarters and further? "It was because of Doss's prayer."

The next day we didn't pray: figured it was an easy mop-up job. That was when our men had to retreat and left approximately seventy-five wounded men on top of the escarpment. They were my men, and I couldn't go off and leave them even if it cost me my life. So I stayed there and let the men down by rope about thirty-five feet to the place where they could be taken by litter to the aid station.

I feel that I received the Congressional Medal of Honor because I kept the Golden Rule that we read in Matthew 7:12: "All things whatsoever ye would that men should do to you, do ye even so to them."

Desmond Doss

*While commanding a machine-gun section, with the enemy overrunning them,
Paige held his position even though all his men were killed or wounded .... Alone,
he continued to fight against overwhelming odds, moving from gun to gun. When
reinforcements arrived he led the bayonet charge that ultimately repulsed the enemy.*

**Sergeant Mitchell Paige, U.S. Marine Corps
Company H, 7th Marine Regiment, 1st Marine Division
October 26, 1942
Solomon Islands**

Mother's Words

I'm often asked the questions, "Why, as a marine, were you willing to put your life on the line for your country?" and "Were you afraid during your battles in the South Pacific in World War II?"

The answers took me back to my childhood, to a small, three-room country school in Pennsylvania where the children were so steeped in the legends and traditions of America they literally felt themselves a part of our glorious heritage. Each day after the bell rang, we marched into our classrooms to the rousing strains of one of John Philip Sousa's marches played on the old upright piano by one of our teachers. Then, as we stood by our desks, the teacher read a verse from the Bible, and we pledged allegiance to the flag of our country, which hung in every classroom, before we sat down for our normal school day.

My parents had admonished me to listen and to learn all I could about this wonderful country, America! They had emigrated from Europe about the turn of the century and fully understood the importance of all the freedoms that so many took for granted. My mother never failed to take me to the patriotic parades where I saw the soldiers, sailors and marines march by with flags flying and bands playing. What a thrill and joy that was!

I will never forget listening to the exciting stories of American history in my school. I learned all about the men who gave their lives to make this country free. We had to memorize all the great documents, such as Lincoln's Gettysburg Address and John Adam's magnificent, spine-tingling speech given on July 4, 1776, in Independence Hall in Philadelphia, when our country was born. I can recite the speech by memory to this day. Every American should and must be familiar with the trials and tribulations experienced by our great Founding Fathers as they established the very bedrock of the United States of America.

This history, with its heroes, is a truly necessary foundation for every American boy and girl. Without this knowledge, how can they understand why our nation became the great country that it is today?

My parents and teachers instilled in me a devout love of God, family and country. So, to respond to those who ask why I was willing to put my life on the line, I answer that "my undying love of country and my strong loyalty to the marines fighting by my side gave me no choice but to fight on unswervingly throughout my battles, utilizing my 'God-given' ability to make use of what I had been taught and what I had learned."

When I left home in 1936 to walk two hundred miles to Baltimore, Maryland, the nearest recruiting station, to join the Marine Corps, my mother's admonition to me, as she handed me my sack lunch, was, "Trust in the Lord, son, and He will guide you always."

These words forever remained in my mind, and whenever fear would overtake me, I was comforted. I will never forget sitting in a foxhole, bloody, burned and injured the morning after our all-night, fierce, hand-to-hand battle against an overwhelming Japanese force on Guadalcanal. ... I was alone, except for hundreds of dead bodies of the enemy surrounding me. I emptied my pack, looking for something to stop the bleeding from a bayonet wound, and out fell my small Bible. Picking it up in my dirty, bloody hands, I could scarcely believe it.

It had providentially opened at Proverbs 3:5–6—and there were my mother's words, "Trust in the Lord with all your heart and lean not on your own understanding; in all your ways acknowledge Him, and He will direct your paths."

Mitchell Paige

... while serving as lead scout trying to free the enemy-encircled city, Biddle advanced alone, separate from his unit, to take out three snipers and three enemy machine-gun positions. At nightfall, he scouted and had two tanks destroyed; at daybreak, he advanced, eliminating a gun position that had pinned down his company, ultimately causing the enemy to flee.

**Private First Class Melvin E. Biddle, U.S. Army
Company B, 517th Parachute Infantry Regiment
December 23–24, 1944
Near Soy, Belgium**

Of War and Roses

I am a golfer who raises roses.

I was a World War II paratrooper who volunteered
for the paratroopers because a girlfriend asked
if I would write her a letter on the way down.

This was the lady I married!

We have been married forty-nine years,
with two daughters and eleven grandchildren.

Melvin Biddle

... seeking refuge in a Belgium factory in Malmédy, the rifleman emerged from cover to engage the enemy hidden in a nearby house, only to discover five Americans trapped within the walls of the German-held house. Realizing only he could save their lives, Currey returned to the streets, launching antitank grenades and firing machine guns, forcing a retreat and allowing the trapped Americans to escape.

Private First Class Francis S. Currey, U.S. Army
Company K, 120th Infantry, 30th Infantry Division
December 21, 1944
Malmédy, Belgium

Of Serendipity ... and Mischance

After we thwarted the German attack on Malmédy, Belgium, on December 21, 1944, we were moved about a mile forward and dug in on a hillside. On the other side of the valley the Germans were dug in.

We stayed in this position almost two weeks before our advance began to eliminate the "Bulge."

While waiting we were able to use a farmhouse about one-half mile behind us a few hours each day to get warm, write letters and get some warm food. The farmhouse was occupied by a Belgian farmer, his wife and a daughter about my age: nineteen.

The Germans would lob a few artillery rounds at us once in a while to let us know they were still there.

One afternoon I was in the farmhouse when the Germans overshot our position, several rounds hitting the farmhouse, the barn and nearby. The girl and I dove into a stairway leading into the cellar. She was underneath me; I was shielding her with my body. After the shelling we got up and the first thing you know, we were kissing—and, of course, nothing more. We moved out a couple weeks later, and I never saw her again.

Fifty years later, in September 1994, my wife and I were with a group of 30th Infantry Division veterans in Belgium, celebrating the 50th anniversary of their liberation. A tremendous celebration was held in Stoumont, Belgium, and thousands of Belgians from the surrounding area turned out for it.

We were walking down a street between the sidewalks lined with Belgians when a woman left the crowd and walked up to me.

"Francis Currey," she said, "I met you in Malmédy in 1944." Then she disappeared back in the crowd.

I was never in Malmédy in 1944; I was always outside of Malmédy. I had received quite a bit of publicity in the local paper, so I thought she was mistaken.

But somehow she seemed familiar. That night at the hotel I realized that she was the girl from the farmhouse in 1944. If only she had mentioned the farmhouse instead of the town, it would have registered. I have no idea what her name is, where she lives or other status.

I would have liked to have talked with her, but it was an opportunity lost—probably never to happen again.

Frank Currey

.... after positioning his six-man team, Morris crawled alone to investigate the enemy positions and instantly was wounded in the chest. After eliminating the immediate enemy, painfully bleeding, he repositioned his men for the ensuing eight-hour battle. Wounded again and again, his left hand now shattered, Morris continued to administer first aid, encouraging his men to defeat the enemy while saving many lives.

Sergeant Charles B. Morris, U.S. Army
Company A, 2d Battalion, 173d Airborne Brigade
June 29, 1966
Republic of Vietnam

I'm But a Custodian

I have always chosen to wear my Medal on the inside instead of wearing it properly. In some ways I was wrong, but since I tried so hard to be "above and beyond" in everything I did as a soldier, perhaps I was able to exert more influence by my example than if I had tried to openly present the hero's image.

You will find very little about me in anything except official records, which is by choice. I have refused to cooperate with the media. Perhaps I'm afraid I might say or do something that might somehow degrade the Medal, or myself as a holder of it.

The Medal is heavy, and it takes a brave man to wear such an awesome award, which not only represents the wearer but the entire nation. I have found that holding the Medal is a humbling experience because it is so much bigger than I will ever be.

I only hold the Medal for the paratroopers of the 173d Airborne Brigade who fought beside me and believed in me, in "sarge." The young soldiers that I led are the heroes, not I.

Please remember that I was a professional soldier and professionals do their job to the best of their ability. If I failed in any way in my career, it was from ignorance and never because I didn't care. My soldiers were important—I was not.

In my career I always felt that if my soldiers failed, then I had failed to teach them. Yes, I counseled them, but I also spent a lot of time with the person responsible, myself, trying to determine where or if I had failed.

I think a lot of people today, including our teachers, government leaders and the media, need to accept full responsibility for their actions, and do some soul searching when things go wrong. They might find the answer to some of our problems in their own hands.

If so, they need the courage to take action.

Charlie Morris

... returning to his platoon after treating heat casualties, Ballard was greeted by enemy fire upon him and his unit. He rendered aid to a wounded marine and as four other marines prepared to move the casualty, he saw a Vietcong soldier throw a grenade toward them. He fearlessly threw himself upon the explosive ... which failed to explode. He eventually arose from his position to continue medically assisting others.

Hospital Corpsman Second Class Donald E. Ballard, U.S. Navy
Company M, 3d Battalion, 4th Marines, 3d Marine Division
May 16, 1968
Quang Tri Province, Vietnam

Problems?

Problems? I don't worry about problems.

All I have to do is visit the Vietnam Wall
to be reminded how precious life is,

Or visit the Veterans Administration hospitals
to realize how little my problems are,

Or to talk with veterans
that mentally haven't made it home yet.

As an American I realize I owe everything to veterans
for the freedoms I enjoy.

Thank God—I have no problems!

"Doc" Don Ballard

The day after leading a successful rescue mission through Chau Phu, Dix assembled a twenty-man force and cleared the Vietcong out of the city's hotel, theater and other adjacent buildings. During the attack, Army Republic of Vietnam soldiers rallied alongside him and began pushing back the enemy. He captured twenty prisoners, including a Vietcong official, and then attacked enemy troops who had entered a high-ranking official's home and rescued the official's wife and children.

Staff Sergeant Drew D. Dix, U.S. Army
U.S. Senior Advisor Group, IV Corps, Military Assistance Command
January 31–February 1, 1968
Chau Doc Province, Vietnam

All Walks of Life

Soon after being awarded the Congressional Medal of Honor, still on active duty, I was asked to attend a dinner in a small town not far from Fort Bragg, North Carolina.

I was reluctant to go since it would interfere with an important military assignment. The Command Sergeant Major said, "Go ahead, you'll enjoy it. There is nothing wrong with having a good time and eating a few shrimp and peanuts." He was very convincing, so I went.

Sure enough there were shrimp and peanuts, and I was having a good time meeting people from this small town. All was going well until we moved to the dining room. I was even escorted to the head table. I thought the Command Sergeant Major really knew what he was talking about—until I looked at the program and read the third line down:

Guest Speaker Drew Dix— "Why Vietnam"—forty-five minutes

Suddenly I wished I'd stayed at Fort Bragg. What would I talk about for forty-five minutes? I'd never talked to a large group like this before, especially people who weren't soldiers. I'd have rather gone through the Medal of Honor action again than to be there at that moment.

The Congressional Medal of Honor doesn't make us an authority on political issues, or any issue for that matter. The public often fails to realize that the Medal of Honor is awarded to people of all walks of life and abilities. This fact alone makes the Congressional Medal of Honor unique.

Drew Dix

... he and three soldiers were occupying a bunker when the enemy threw in three explosive charges. Quickly Fitzmaurice threw out two, then hurled his bulletproof vest and body over the remaining charge. He absorbed the full blast to shield his comrades. Wounded, his sight half gone, he left his position and charged the enemy ... .

**Specialist Fourth Class Michael John Fitzmaurice, U.S. Army
Troop D, 2d Squadron, 17th Cavalry, 101st Airborne Division
March 23, 1971
Khesanh, Vietnam**

Peace on Earth

I remember we were stationed at Camp Eagle, Vietnam, in 1970. It was Christmas Eve and as it happened, every night someone went out on ambush. This night I was along.

We wait until dark and then head out to the graveyard outside of the camp and set up to ambush the enemy. It's raining like crazy. We are all cold and wet, when this helicopter starts flying around Camp Eagle playing Christmas songs, something with "Peace on Earth, Goodwill toward Men."

It has now been twenty-five years, and that Christmas in Vietnam is still as clear today as it was then.

Funny what you remember ...

Peace on Earth and Goodwill toward Men ... .

Michael Fitzmaurice

... during intense fog, smoke and gunfire, Brady continued to fly ambulance helicopters, mission after mission, evacuating the wounded from the embattled landing zone, where other pilots before him had been shot down. So severe was the battle and the destruction to his own aircraft, he had to use three different helicopters to evacuate fifty-one seriously wounded men.

Major Patrick Henry Brady, U.S. Army
Medical Service Corps, 54th Medical Detachment,
67th Medical Group, 44th Medical Brigade
January 6, 1968
Near Chu Lai, Vietnam

The Equalizer

Over the years I have become convinced
that the key to just about everything is courage.
Not only the combat type (which is mostly overrated),
but the moral type.

Why courage?
Because we are not born equal in terms of ability or opportunity.
There is only one way we are equal
and can compete equally in life: courage!

Each of us can have all the courage we want—
it's the great equalizer in life. It produces great people
from those not born with great ability or opportunity.

And where does it come from?
What's the key?
The answer is "faith"— and you can define that as you wish,
but essentially it "takes us beyond a particular moment,
above and beyond the self."

Major General Patrick Brady

… during an intense battle, finding his commander dying and the key personnel and radio operator dead, Barnum strapped on the radio assuming command. In the midst of the attack while fully exposed to the enemy, he organized a stinging counterattack. Though his units were decimated, he motivated his men by exposing himself to the deadly fire, pinpointing targets, calling in armed helicopters and securing a landing zone to evacuate the dead and wounded.

**First Lieutenant Harvey C. Barnum, Jr., U.S. Marine Corps
Company H, 2d Battalion, 9th Marines, 3d Marine Division
December 18, 1965
Ky Phu, Quang Tin Province, Vietnam**

Cheshire High

It was Military Day at Cheshire High School, Cheshire, Connecticut, and the military service representatives were attempting to recruit students into their respective branches. The junior and senior boys assembled in the school auditorium with faculty members observing from the rear of the room as each recruiter got up to give his pitch.

The Air Force recruiter got up to explain the advantages of joining the United States Air Force. He was greeted with catcalls and whistles from the young high schoolers. ... The Army recruiter received the same treatment, as did the Navy recruiter. The Marine recruiter, a seasoned gunnery sergeant, rose and glared at the assembled students. "There is no one here worthy of being a United States Marine," he growled. "I deplore the fact that the faculty in the back of the room would let the students carry on like this. There isn't anybody here I want in my Marine Corps."

When he sat down, several eager students swarmed around his table. I was one of them. I was so impressed with the "gunny's" sense of discipline, professionalism and total dedication to his high standards that I did the paperwork to enlist as a senior in high school and later joined the Platoon Leadership Program, an officer program, when I got to St. Anselm College in New Hampshire.

I served thirty years as an officer in the Marines. That Marine Corps Gunnery Sergeant taught me several lessons:

Leaders must be highly disciplined.

They know they can't control others if they can't first control themselves.

They set strict priorities for themselves and resist the temptation to engage in nonproductive pursuits.

Good leaders always set the example.

They do what is right regardless of consequences, always maintaining the high standards they have set.

The gunny didn't adjust himself to the unruly behavior of the students who didn't share his view of the Marine Corps and its mission. He didn't drop to their standards. He eliminated them from consideration. He ignored the easy way of adjusting to mediocrity. He was strong, decisive and firm. His actions so impressed me I wanted to be like him—A United States Marine!

H. C. "Barney" Barnum, Jr.
Colonel of Marines (Retired)

... Lang was serving as the squad leader when his unit encountered intense fire from three enemy bunker emplacements. He maneuvered from one position to the other, destroying them with grenades and rifle fire, until suddenly his unit was surrounded by heavy enemy rocket and automatic weapons fire ... six men were hit, including himself. Although immobilized, he continued directing his men until his own evacuation was ordered over his protest.

Specialist Fourth Class George C. Lang, U.S. Army
Company A, 4th Battalion, 47th Infantry, 9th Infantry Division
February 22, 1969
Kien Hoa Province, Vietnam

Miracles Do Happen

It's hard getting started. The day I was wounded is a pretty amazing story. After I blew up the last bunker, a B-40 rocket landed somewhere around me and sent me flying. A piece of shrapnel caught me in the back about even with my bellybutton, severing my spine. I was conscious, but surprisingly had no pain.

I called for a medic because I couldn't move. When the medic came, he checked me and asked, "Where are you hit?" I said, "I don't know, but I can't move." He started bandaging my wrists, which had blown out in the concussion. In a split second he was shot in the hands and went back to get aid. I kept yelling for another medic; meanwhile, it seemed like everybody was running out of ammo at the same time, so I told my men to let every other man fire so there would be constant firing.

I don't know how long I was lying there, but I felt a little cold so I put my arm over my chest and seconds later got hit with a bullet in the elbow that blew open my forearm and went up my biceps and just missed my head. It looked terrible; I just put it down by my side. The surprising thing was I had no pain.

A few hours later some men got up to where I was and pulled me back to the command post. We were in a wooded area, and the command post was near a large bunker they were using to land small helicopters on to evacuate the wounded.

A helicopter landed on top of the bunker, one guy stood me up and had my head and shoulders in the helicopter, and another guy went around to the other side to pull me in.

The helicopter started to tilt, and the blades were getting close to the ground, so they started to pull up—just then the guy holding me and I both fell off the helicopter, dropping about ten feet—and again, no pain.

The helicopter landed again, and I told two other guys that were wounded to get in and I'll wait for the next one.

This entire time I was conscious and didn't have any pain. All I knew was that God was there watching over me. He was the one who took away the pain.

Miracles do happen, and I'm living proof!

George Lang

... as he landed with the first assault wave on the beaches of the Gulf of Salerno, Logan faced a serious counterattack along an inland canal. He eliminated the first three Germans who challenged him, then crawled along the foot of the canal's wall, hurdled it and grabbing an enemy machine gun, opened fire on those attempting to flee. He captured an enemy officer and soldier and soon after shot a sniper in a nearby house.

Sergeant James M. Logan, U.S. Army
Company I, 3d Battalion, 141st Infantry, 36th Infantry Division
September 9, 1943
Near Salerno, Italy

Taking the Town

I've always maintained that it was the Great Depression that helped me survive World War II.

Things were tough at home before I went to war. I was used to hunting rabbits and squirrels so my family could eat. I guess that made me pretty good with a gun.

The morning after the battle for which I was awarded the Medal of Honor, I left my company, heading out alone before daylight. I slipped down the highway and sneaked into the German-held town of Agrapoli, the town we were supposed to take.

By the time my entire company made it to the town, I had already been drinking wine and getting a shave and haircut from an Italian shopkeeper. I guess you could say I took the town myself.

People always ask me how I dodged all those bullets. Well, I just tell 'em there weren't many bird, squirrel or rabbit hunters among that bunch we were fighting.

James Logan

... while on an aerial photographic mapping mission, Zeamer and his crew came under attack by about twenty enemy fighter planes from the airfield below. Shot in both arms and legs, he maneuvered his plane skillfully throughout a forty-minute fight in which he and his crew destroyed at least five of the hostile planes, until the enemy broke contact, and he directed his aircraft to a base nearly six hundred miles away.

Captain Jay Zeamer, Jr., U.S. Army Air Corps
65th Bombardment Squadron, 43d Bombardment Group, 5th Air Force
June 16, 1943
Over Buka, Solomon Islands

A Symbol of Their Spirit

For every Medal of Honor awarded
there are many instances of heroism not observed
or not reported or not written up.

Whenever I wear my Medal,
I can't help thinking of these men
and considering my Medal as representative
and symbolic of them, they who received no recognition
except, in some cases, a posthumous Purple Heart.

There is a certain quality and spirit bred into Americans
that causes them, under certain situations,
to spontaneously take necessary action—regardless.
I feel it is important to keep the concept of the Medal alive
in support of this spirit
and to pass it on to future generations.

Jay Zeamer, Jr.

After eliminating four of an enemy patrol, he crawled forward under fire, chased off the enemy mortar section and took over a machine-gun position. The next day, when the platoon was forced to withdraw, Ehlers diverted the bulk of the heavy hostile fire to himself to allow his squad to withdraw safely. Though wounded, he carried a fellow soldier to safety and even returned to the shell-swept field to retrieve his weapon.

Staff Sergeant Walter D. Ehlers, U.S. Army
18th Infantry, 1st Infantry Division
June 9–10, 1944
Near Goville, France

A Mother's Request

When I enlisted in the army, my mother said, "If you are going to be a soldier, be a Christian soldier." I assured her I would do my best, so she signed the permission for my enlistment. Every time I was tempted to do some crazy thing, I remembered what my mother had told me.

I carried my New Testament of the Bible and read the Twenty-third Psalm many times. The Ten Commandments and the Lord's Prayer were my salvation. *"Leadeth not into temptation but delivereth us from evil"* has come to my aid many times.

If you do not believe in God, you have no one to answer to. When you do believe in God, you resist evil temptations, and you are delivered from evil.

During combat in Germany, I was wounded, and at some point when my pack was removed, I lost my New Testament.

About ten years after the war, my mother received a package from a German woman. It included my Bible and a letter from the woman explaining that her children had found the Bible under some rocks behind her house. She wrote that she was returning the Bible to my mother since her name and address were in it, and that she hoped Walter had returned home safely. In any case, she thought the Bible would be a comfort to my mother.

Mother was thrilled to receive the Bible. She could tell by the thumbing of the pages that it had been well used. My mother was my inspiration, and her leading me to God was my salvation. Being a "Christian soldier" has many rewards.

Walter D. Ehlers

... armed with only minimum weapons, Rosser charged enemy positions, three times reloading his ammunition supply between charges, while losing every one of the comrades with him to Korean fire. Hurling grenades, he crested the hill for the third time, destroyed thirteen enemies, several bunkers and removed his injured comrades to safety.

Corporal Ronald E. Rosser, U.S. Army
Headquarters Company, 38th Infantry Regiment, 2d Infantry Division
January 12, 1952
Near Ponggilli, Korea

Children of War

One of the first things I noticed
in the war zone was the children.
They were all trying to survive
the best way they could.

I picked up one orphan
and made him the platoon houseboy.
I felt I needed to save at least one.

Wouldn't it be nice if the people who start wars
had to raise the orphans of that war?

Ron Rosser

... as a medical corpsman, braving the fury of Japanese artillery and mortar and machine-gun fire, Bush fearlessly moved from one casualty to another, providing medical assistance. As the savage attack passed over the ridge, the eighteen year old, fully exposed to the enemy, held high in one hand a blood plasma bottle to save a marine officer while using his free hand to fire his pistol and a discarded carbine into the charging Japanese. He suffered wounds of his own, losing an eye, but refused medical treatment until the officer was evacuated.

Hospital Apprentice First Class Robert E. Bush, U.S. Naval Reserve
2d Battalion, 5th Marines, 1st Marine Division
May 2, 1945
Okinawa Jima, Ryukyu Islands

Count Your Blessings

My sister and I were raised by my mother. She was a single parent, working as a registered nurse. We lived in the basement of the Bridge clinic, a thirty-bed hospital in Raymond, Washington. We ate whatever food was on the trays back then, so the environment was not very family oriented. We were very poor.

By the time I got to the eighth grade, my mother had remarried. I attended the Willapa Valley High School in Menlo, Washington. When I came home from school, my mother was still at work. That gave me plenty of opportunity to get in all kinds of trouble.

But I had a coach at school named Ed Tenonski. He took me under his wing and turned me around.

At age seventeen, most of the boys in our high school were already in the service fighting for our country in World War II. I elected to join the navy in my junior year, rather than finish school. I figured I would do that when I returned home. That's exactly what I did.

When you grow up like I did, you realize the value of an education. At age nineteen, married and after receiving the nation's highest award, I finally graduated from Valley High in 1946. After furthering my education, I founded the Bayview Lumber Company in 1951, and to this day I still serve as president of the organization.

I have been fortunate to have a number of mentors in life who influenced me tremendously. As you know now, I admired my high school coach Ed Tenonski. He always had me say, "You practice like you play." I listened intensively to him, and he prepared me for the life ahead.

The second quotation that has stuck with me came from Ernie Pyle on Okinawa, when that great war correspondent stated that "the war is only one hundred yards on both sides of you," allowing me to concentrate on the task at hand.

A third memorable quotation was from General Jimmy Doolittle, who was the master of the calculated risk. He taught me to calculate the risk in whatever you are doing in life and react accordingly.

I'm very proud of my service to my country, but I am most proud of my patriotic and productive family. The greatest assets I developed over the years are my four children, nine grandchildren and six great-grandchildren.

The last and most recent quotation I would like to share is from Dolly Parton, who said, "Don't count your money, count your blessings."

My wife, Wanda, and I are indeed blessed.

Bob Bush

... during Japan's infamous attack on Pearl Harbor, Ross's station in the USS Nevada's forward dynamo room suddenly filled with choking smoke and lethal heat and steam. He forced his men to leave, then performed all the duties himself until blinded and unconscious. As soon as Ross was rescued and resuscitated, he returned to secure his station as well as its duplicate immediately to the rear. Again losing consciousness and being revived, he staunchly remained on duty until the captain directed the crew to abandon ship.

Warrant Machinist Donald K. Ross, U.S. Navy
USS *Nevada*
December 7, 1941
Pearl Harbor, Territory of Hawaii

Half of a Crazy Pair

We were a crazy pair. Especially Don; alone he could make up a whole pair. As a friend said after listening to one of his salty tales, "Don Ross, you are—too much!"

People are naturally curious about how a couple met, particularly when the creaky, wrinkled, sagging couple limp toward their golden wedding anniversary.

When asked how WE met, Don Ross often replied, "Helen picked me out of the gutter." I must admit, there was some truth in it.

What gutter? Downtown Honolulu, September 16, 1940. My roommate and I strolled up Fort Street with our dates. We had just left the post office, en route to meeting my date's mother.

A handsome, dry-behind-the-ears man came swinging down the sidewalk, whistling a tune. Usually, good-looking men didn't impress me, but this one did. From his shirt pocket he took a small piece of paper; a sudden breeze snatched it, depositing it in the gutter.

As he stooped to retrieve the paper, he turned and looked up. Oh! Those twinkly eyes! Wow! My date came to a halt, as did I.

"Well, Don, what are you doing in the gutter?"

Twinkly Eyes grinned. "Your mother needs a money order, and I'm on my way to the post office." His eyes looked straight at me and everything in my chest flip-flopped. Well, perhaps I'm stretching it a bit. Later they said I whispered when I asked, "WHO was THAT?"

Bob nudged my elbow. "Nobody. Just another sailor."

Four blocks later, Bob's mother surprised us by announcing she would join our dinner party and her date would be Don Ross.

I don't recall a thing about our dinner or my date, "Bob" (I had to make up his name, in writing this). Don and I danced; he drove me home. And, yes, you might say, I stole someone else's date—for good.

We were married a month after the attack on Pearl Harbor. Between those two momentous occasions, Don was hospitalized for treatment to his eyes, which were dimmed by December seven's inferno. The nights were cool, and the skimpy hospital gowns and shortage of blankets prompted Don to request my Uncle Fred's long red-flannel nightgown, which my mother had wrapped as a gift for him.

Ever the entertainer, he donned the robe, dancing, wildly swaying, anything to bring a smile to the other patients. It wasn't long before he overheard a doctor and nurse discuss him and Section Eight, the military's discharge for mental illness. The next step? Surveyed out of the navy.

No way! He had no clothing of his own; his bedroom slippers and the filthy clothes in which he'd fought had rotted away from oil and saltwater. But Don Ross hadn't been in the navy for eleven years for nothing.

It didn't take him long to outfit himself in a laundry room. He strode through the hospital door and hurried down the path to fetch a ride to Waipio Point, where BB-36 waited for him on the beach.

The officer of the day saluted. "Mr. Ross, where are your orders?"

"My orders? Oh, yes. They were too busy at the hospital. Absolutely wild. You can't imagine. But don't worry. My orders will come when they get around to it."

To Don's knowledge, no one missed him or reported his sudden departure. As far as he knew, his orders never did come. Everyone was glad to see another person willing to help with the horrible job of salvaging the sinking ship.

Perhaps you know the rest: the march up the rating from recruit to Junior Warrant; the Medal of Honor; Puget Sound Navy Yard in Bremerton for repairs; Chief Warrant (his dream), then Ensign (his nightmare); Battle of the Aleutians, Atlantic Convoy; D-day off the coast of northern France; bombardment of southern France; back to Norfolk for both ship repairs and Don. Then two separate double-hernia surgeries at the Great Lakes, followed by months of public affairs work. He enjoyed working with the public but felt it was time wasted.

When kamikazes hit the *Nevada* in the spring of 1945, he knew he had to get to HIS ship. He called the Bureat requesting orders. They didn't come fast enough. So he packed his bag, hopped a train for San Francisco and boarded a navy ship bound for Pearl. Once there, he found chaos in the engineering department. Up in the skipper's cabin, Admiral Grosskopf roared, "And who the hell are you?"

You know that old saw? "My order will follow." Grosskopf bit—and Ross went back where he belonged, back with the Black Gang.

I wonder now, if those readers who knew retired Captain Don Ross as a portly, well-behaved, mature country gentleman can identify with this fun-loving character who seldom took "NO" for an answer. What COULD be done, would be done.

Yes, it is true, Don Ross was some kind of a crazy character. I look back on those fifty years with great fondness.

We were a crazy pair. And it was fun!

Helen Ross,
remembering her husband,
Don Ross

... Benavidez voluntarily boarded a returning helicopter with crewmembers who were wounded while trying to rescue a twelve-man team in the dense jungle, under heavy attack and pinned down, west of Loc Ninh. He alone was dropped into the area, and although wounded numerous times, took command, called in air strikes and carried and dragged the wounded to safety for pick up by helicopters. He saved the lives of eight men.

Staff Sergeant Roy P. Benavidez, U.S. Army
Detachment B-56, 5th Special Forces Group (Airborne),
1st Special Forces
May 2, 1968
Near Loc Ninh, Vietnam

Hold On

I was born outside of Quero, Texas, in a village called Lindeneau. When I was six and my brother was five, our parents died and as a custom of Hispanic Americans, my father's brother, our uncle Nick, and his family of eight children adopted us as their own.

Half the year we would go to school, and the other half we were migrant workers, picking cotton and sugar beets from Texas to Colorado. During high school I was on the wrestling and boxing teams. But I dropped out of school, something I'm not proud of and would never recommend. I continued to work in my neighboring area, but I was told that an education and a diploma were the keys to success. And that bad habits and bad company would ruin a person.

So I needed an education and a skill; that's when I joined the Texas National Guard. Shortly afterwards came my induction into the regular army and my high school diploma. From there I went to the 82d Airborne, then on to the Green Beret Special Forces. I had a total of twenty-five years in the military.

After my military career, I enrolled in our county junior college, majoring in speech. After receiving the Congressional Medal of Honor, I knew I would be asked to speak at many events, so I chose public speaking as a course of study.

As it happened, I did go on the speaking tour, and I continue to this day. My very first was the United States Military Academy at West Point, speaking before four thousand cadets. But my most memorable engagements are usually at schools—and one in particular stands out among the rest.

I was speaking at a high school in the valley of Texas. After the presentation, an ROTC instructor came to me with congratulations, telling me what a wonderful and inspirational speech I had given, especially the points about the keys to success being education and a diploma, plus incorporating a positive attitude and having faith in one's self.

But, he told me, there's one cadet over there, Linda, who's about to quit the program and school to run off and get married. He wondered if I'd take the time to talk with her.

Immediately I walked over to her and with concern said, "Cadet." "Yes sir," she said. "What are you going to do when you graduate?" Her reply was, "I want to get married, so I'm going to quit school." "If you don't quit school," I said, "you can be anything you want to if you just try. What is it that you want?" She answered, "I want to be a court recorder and interpreter." My response was instantaneous: "Linda, let me tell you about my grandfather." His story always helped keep me going in life. I'll never forget his words, "Hold on … I'll help you!"

Grandfather was born and lived his life in Mexico. One day he was leading a herd of cows down a road and as he approached a bend, he heard someone yelling, "Help, help!" A man had fallen off a cliff by the side of the road and was hanging onto a tree stump for his life.

Grandfather grabbed a rope tied around one of the cows and lowered it down the cliff, but it was too short and couldn't reach the man. He yelled to the man, "Hold on, hold on!"

Quickly he took off his belt and tied it on to the end of the rope, again lowering it down to the man. This time it was long enough. Grandfather said again, "Hold on, hold on, I'll help you!" The man just barely grabbed the rope, and Granddad pulled him up.

"Linda," I said, "just hold on and get that diploma."

Almost ten years went by, when I was speaking at a Hispanic American Conference in Chicago. After the speech a young woman came up to me and asked, "May I hug you?" She was crying, she was so moved; I was wondering who she was. She said, "You don't remember me, do you?" So I queried, "Well, where are you from?" and she told me, "The valley in Texas."

And it all came tumbling out. "In the valley, you came to speak at my high school, when I was about to quit school and get married, but you told me the story about your grandfather, 'Hold on!'"

"I did graduate from high school and the University of Texas. I now work for the State of Illinois as a court recorder and interpreter. Thanks to you I did 'hold on,' and now I'm living my dream."

Roy Benavidez
Author, Medal of Honor:
A Vietnam Warrior's Story

… Millett personally led the remainder of his company over a fire-swept hill in the face of the enemy, using fixed bayonets and whirlwind hand-to-hand attacks to free his first platoon being pinned down … although wounded, he refused medical evacuation until the enemy wildly fled.

Captain Lewis Lee "Red" Millett, U.S. Army
Company E, 27th Infantry Regiment, 25th Infantry Division
February 7, 1951
Near Soam-Ni, Korea

Freedom

If I'm a slave and you are free, will you fight for my liberty?

An Old Soldier's Prayer

I have fought when others feared to serve.
I have gone where others failed to go.
I've lost friends in war and strife,
Who valued Duty more than love of life.

I have shared the comradeship of pain.
I've searched the lands for men that we've lost.
I have sons who served this land of liberty,
Who'd fight to insure other stricken lands are free.

I have seen the weak forsake humanity.
I have heard the traitors praise our enemy.
I've seen challenged men become ever bolder.
I've seen the duty, honor, sacrifice of the soldier.

Now I understand the meaning of our lives.
The loss of comrades not so very long ago.
So to you who've answered duty's siren call.
May God Bless you, my son, may God Bless you all.

Mountain Reverie

The dark, green conifers reach for the sky,
While beneath the oaks brown acorns lie.
A massive rock rears upward, too,
glistening white with the morning dew.

Low, scudding clouds brush across the scene,
Tracing the forest with a moisture skein.
While coons, squirrels and other creatures,
Make this one of nature's beautiful features.

The forest floor is covered with needles of pine,
While falling snow blankets the mountain's spine.
The soft snow falls gently on the forest green,
Bringing quiet tranquillity to this mountain scene.

Holiday greetings trip through my mind,
So Peace and God Bless you to all Mankind.

Lewis Millett

... with his small patrol outnumbered, Murray observed two hundred Germans pouring deadly mortar, bazooka and machine-gun fire on an American battalion. Rather than risk the lives of his patrol, he crawled out ahead to the enemy to call in artillery fire until his radio went dead. At his self-appointed outpost, he fired on the enemy, killing and wounding them as they began to withdraw, and although wounded by a grenade blast, Murray eventually captured eleven enemy soldiers.

**First Lieutenant Charles P. Murray, Jr., U.S. Army
Company C, 30th Infantry, 3d Infantry Division,
December 16, 1944
Kaysersberg, France**

Stretch Your Limits

As I look back over the years of my life, it becomes clear that education and training have always been important to me. To these areas I have always assigned a high priority.

Even in the elementary grades, I worked to do the best I could and to gain from the opportunities which came my way. As early as the sixth grade, I was recognized for my efforts by the local America Legion post, which presented me with a certificate. Outside of school, I devoted much of my free time to the public library, taking home and reading great books purely for pleasure.

This trend continued throughout my high school years. I received generally high grades and was inducted into the National Honor Society in my senior year.

During these early years, although I was a good student, my life was not solely limited to studies. In the difficult times before World War II, I began selling magazines at age eight, then newspapers on a downtown corner and later got a newspaper delivery route. At a very young age, I was streetwise, sometimes even combative. I participated in field and track competitions in elementary school, but in high school I didn't strive to become a member of any athletic team. However, I was interested in sports and was an assistant manager of the football team and manager of the boxing team.

My training with weapons started early, too. When I was ten, I was entrusted with my grandfather's single-shot 22 rifle and was permitted to hunt game birds on my own. Four years later, my father gave me a 410-gauge shotgun, and it was with this weapon that I learned to shoot quail. It wasn't easy at all to hit a target on the wing with this small gun, but with practice, I could do just that. After I proved my ability to handle the weapon and showed that I understood the safety rules, I began to hunt on my own.

The training and experience with that 22 and the 410 served me well when I entered the army. Shooting was almost second nature to me, and I qualified expert with most weapons then available in infantry units.

The Boy Scouts of America was another training ground that served me well. I joined the Scouts as soon as I reached the minimum age of twelve and stayed active in scouting until I went off to college. My years in the Scouts instilled in me several vital traits: love of country; respect for our flag; assistance to others; self-discipline; leadership; community service and citizenship.

The Scout training also taught me a number of skills that helped me perform in the army too, not the least of which was the ability to hike and live in the field. I learned the rudiments of leadership through successive assignments as assistant patrol leader, patrol leader, senior patrol leader and junior assistant scoutmaster. However, I still regret I didn't attain the rank of Eagle.

I strongly recommend that every young American join the scouting program and participate fully in the organization's activities. And I most certainly salute anyone who attains or has already attained the rank of Eagle Scout, or the equivalent in the Girl Scouts of America.

My academic education continued after high school and continues today. My studies at the University of North Carolina at Chapel Hill were interrupted after my third year when I entered the army in 1942. It was at least in part due to my educational background that I was selected early for officer candidate school.

After the end of World War II, I left active duty in September 1945 and returned to Chapel Hill to complete the requirements for my degree. As soon as this goal had been achieved, I applied for regular army and returned to active duty in September 1946.

While on active duty, I grasped at opportunities to further my education. Over the years I attended the Infantry Officers Career Course, Parachute School, Armed Forces Information School, Canadian Army Staff College and the National War College. While attending the National War College, I enrolled in George Washington University, went to night classes and earned a Masters Degree in International Affairs in 1964.

Even today my interest in education continues. I regularly take advantage of opportunities provided by my proximity to the University of South Carolina to attend seminars and other presentations in the field of international relations and world events.

My admonishment to the youth of America is to take maximum advantage of every opportunity that comes your way to advance yourself through education and training.

Moreover, you should search for ways to do this, not just wait for opportunity to come knocking. And in all things, always do your best—and even beyond this, work hard to do better and stretch the limits you consider your maximums.

Along with this personal goal, you should always strive to be a decent, law-abiding, contributing member of your local community, your state and your nation: a good citizen of America.

Charles P. Murray

Frank Sigler with grandson Derrick Peter at Parris Island, South Carolina, October 2, 1992.

... voluntarily taking over command of his rifle squad during the battle of Iwo Jima, Sigler led a charge against Japanese who had been stalling his unit's advance for days. He scaled rocks, surprising the enemy with heavy fire ... although wounded himself, he aided others, including three comrades he carried to safety before returning to the battle, where he held out until ordered to get medical treatment.

Private Franklin E. Sigler, U.S. Marine Corps Reserve
Company F, 2d Battalion, 26th Marines, 5th Marine Division
March 14, 1945
Iwo Jima, Volcano Islands

Our Dad, the Humble Hero

In memory of Father one must speak of what was most important to him: his family. He was born to Elsie and George Sigler, had four brothers and one sister. The brothers shared a close bond. As for Frank's sister, she has said that she had six fathers: her natural and five brothers.

Frank married Virginia Helen Seaman. They enjoyed forty-seven years of marriage and bore two daughters. He was a devoted father and tended to his elder Aunt Mame. He always made time for his daughters to play softball, ride bicycles, swim, go for rides in the country, take walks in the forest and teach them to respect animals. With a love for farming, it was not uncommon to see him in his large vegetable garden with his two daughters in tow. In later years, he had a smaller vegetable garden with two grandsons in tow. Family life included long and laborious drives to Arizona from New Jersey to visit his parents on their cattle ranch.

He had no falsehoods, was charitable and compassionate. He strived to give others recognition rather than take credit for his own deeds. Frank's comment when he was invited to the Fifty Year Celebration for the Battle of Iwo Jima was: "Give the recognition to the younger veterans." Attending his grandson's graduation from the Marine Corps boot camp, he was interviewed by a reporter. The printed article included a photo caption with him and his grandson. Frank was so proud of his grandson that this picture became the only one he would give to fans.

Upon Frank Sigler's death in January 1995, his mother Elsie requested that her son be laid to rest at Arlington National Cemetery near his brother Bill who was killed in World War II, Pacific Campaign. After nearly fifty years, space remained and the brothers rest side by side. A few weeks after Frank's death, a unique experience happened to one of his family members. His presence was felt so strongly one night that this family member was certain he was delivering a message to "take care of her." Although Mrs. Sigler's illness was not noticeable at the time, weeks later she became ill and was diagnosed with cancer. Those who knew him would agree that, if possible, Frank would speak from the grave to nurture his family. The one thing we know for certain he would tell us: Take care of each other, and sempre fidelis.

Presented with love by his daughters,
Susan Francis Sigler Peter *and* **Betty Lee Sigler**

... as the leader of a marine fighter squadron flying Grumman F-4F Wildcats in aerial combat, although vastly outnumbered and suffering from extreme physical and mental strain, Galer personally shot down eleven enemy bomber and fighter aircraft in but twenty-nine days ... .

Major Robert E. Galer, U.S. Marine Corps
Marine Fighter Squadron 244, Aviation Group 21
October 1, 1942
Over the Solomon Islands

Faith

Believe in God, have faith in His teachings
and always perform to His Commandments,
and you should have a wonderful life.
He is always with you!

I've been shot up and shot down four times.
God always had someone there to help.

Once it was the marines, once the Australian Coast Watchers
and another time a naval helicopter pilot,
who picked me up one hundred miles deep in enemy territory.
I was at Pearl Harbor during the bombing, and I made three D-day landings—at
Iwo Jima, in the Philippines and on Okinawa.

I never met an atheist when under fire!

Follow His Commandments, and He will take care of you.

R. E. Galer
Brigadier General, USMC

... during a fierce night attack, Dewey and his assistant gunner were receiving medical attention for their wounds when an enemy lobbed a grenade into his position. Though intensely suffering, Dewey threw the medic to the ground, warned the other marines, then selflessly smothered the grenade with his own body ... absorbing the blast's full force to save the lives of his comrades.

Corporal Duane E. Dewey, U.S. Marine Corps Reserve
Company E, 2d Battalion, 5th Marines, 1st Marine Division
April 16, 1952
Near Panmunjon, Korea

Like What You Do

I do feel my biggest joy in my life is my wife of forty-five years, our two children, our two grandsons and the many friends that we have.

When I came out of the marines in 1952, I had a ninth grade education and was trying to get a job in a piano factory. The personnel man asked me what I learned in the marines and I told him: I was really good with a machine gun and could throw a hand grenade forty or fifty yards. He told me they didn't need that kind of talent but hired me anyway.

After seven long hard years, disliking every minute I worked there, I quit and went to trade school to learn office machine repair. After I finished the eighteen-month course, I started my own office machine service and sales. I had a very successful business.

Just goes to show what you can do in this great country of ours with a little determination and the will to work and a good wife, like the one that helped me all the way.

If I had a message for young people today, it would be to study hard and get an education and whatever you do, do your best and like what you do!

Duane Dewey

... as a tank commander, Burt's unit encountered murderous small-arms and mortar fire. He jumped from his tank and, moving on foot, exposed himself to the enemy to direct the tanks' fire. He was wounded in the face and neck, but this did not keep him from holding the combined forces together for the next eight days of battle. Twice, tanks he rode on were knocked out by the enemy, but he would mount another and continue to fight, all the while rescuing his wounded comrades.

Captain James M. Burt, U.S. Army
Company B, 66th Armored Regiment, 2d Armored Division
October 13, 1944
Near Wurselen, Germany

Life's Helpers

Trust is #1. Horizontal and vertical. ... Humor is #1.
Long, short, light, heavy and daily ...
even macabre humor.

Visibility is #1. Share yourself daily, often ...
never with a disturbed attitude.

Savvy or Experience is #1. All that has been learned,
assembled, coordinated and used.

ESP helps!

During my life, I received an academic and football scholarship in the depression; earned the degrees of Bachelor of Science in Chemistry, a Master of Education, a Master of Military Science; participated in seven campaigns and three invasions during World War II; worked in the paper industry for twenty-one years, taught for eleven years and was a househusband for five.

Now I'm busy growing berries, boulders and deer in New Hampshire; stove wood, gypsy moths and deer in Pennsylvania; and pine, peanuts and deer in Georgia.

James M. Burt

... as a demolition expert, Williams volunteered to go forward alone to try to reduce the devastating enemy machine-gun fire holding his unit down. He fought desperately for four hours, covered by only four riflemen, maneuvering from enemy position to position to silence them, then returning to get more demolition charges and flamethrowers. At one point Williams inserted the nozzle of his flamethrower through an air vent to flush a pillbox, then with a burst of flame, eliminated the charging enemy.

**Corporal Hershel W. Williams, U.S. Marine Corps Reserve
Headquarters Company, 21st Marines, 3d Marine Division
February 23, 1945
Iwo Jima, Volcano Islands**

Why Me?

When I was fifteen years old, I hitched a ride with a man from our community driving a convertible car. He began speeding; my pleading did no good. The car failed to make a sharp curve and clipped off an electric pole, causing me to be thrown from the car. I had no broken bones but was cut and peeled all over. Most of my clothes were torn off. I wondered at the time and for years later why was I not killed.

Then came along World War II. I was really too short to get in the marines, but because of the war, I was permitted to join. One day I found myself on a little island called Iwo Jima. I was one of seventeen who was still living out of my original company. I was always confident I would not die, but I kept wondering why I was permitted to live when so many of my buddies didn't.

On November 5, 1945, on the White House lawn, my life changed. I realized for the first time I was receiving a medal, an award, on behalf of those who didn't make it. They had made it possible for me to be there.

I still couldn't understand "Why me?"

On May 2, 1961, my life changed again. For the first time, I fully realized that God had had a hand in my surviving the automobile crash and the war—and for the first time, I understood why I was permitted to live. He wanted me to do His work, to be part of His world.

Hershel Woody Williams

... acting without orders, the sergeant alone was responsible for eliminating nearly one hundred Germans as his company continued to be attacked and overrun by infantry and tanks. Lopez miraculously charged from position to position, firing his gun until his ammunition was spent and his company was able to advance on to Krinkelt.

Sergeant Jose M. Lopez, U.S. Army
Company M, 23d Infantry, 2d Infantry Division
December 17, 1944
Near Krinkelt, Belgium

Family and Faith

Throughout my life I have realized that the only way to survive in life is with Family and Faith.

I feel as though family and faith are the key to survival because without both, we would not be where we are or who we are today.

It's thanks to my family that I am Jose M. Lopez, Congressional Medal of Honor winner, and Jose M. Lopez, husband, father and grandfather. It's thanks to my faith that I am with my family today. During wars, rough times or any time, I always relied on my faith, for it was my faith that pulled me through.

Today, at eighty-five, I spend all my time with my lovely wife, my wonderful children and my energetic and vibrant grandchildren. In addition to spending time with my family, I also pray, attend church and do everything possible to keep my faith alive.

With these few words, I hope you understand how lucky you are to have family around—and I hope you understand how important it is to have faith as well—because without both, truly, where would we be and who would we be?

Jose M. Lopez

... Tominac burst across open land, his machine gun blaring, quieted an enemy stronghold and then led his squad to eliminate a second enemy group. Afterwards, while advancing ahead of his men to a third enemy position, he was wounded and his support tank began rolling downhill, unmanned toward the enemy. Despite enemy fire and the tank engulfed in flames, Tominac immediately climbed the turret and poured its antiaircraft fire into the enemy until they withdrew. Jumping from the burning tank as it exploded beneath his feet, he continued a direct assault that forced thirty-two Germans to surrender.

First Lieutenant John J. Tominac, U.S. Army
Company I, 15th Infantry, 3d Infantry Division
September 12, 1944
Saulx de Vesoul, France

Indispensable Traits

At the risk of oversimplifying one's struggles in life, I can confirm without hesitation or reservation the truth of the saying, "No pain, no gain." Whether it was taking an objective on the battlefields of Europe during World War II, or pursuing an endeavor in the private sector, the level of success achieved invariably can be measured by the degree of pain and sacrifice that we willingly committed to the task.

I grew up in an extremely friendly, but economically depressed, neighborhood comprised of immigrant families from many different ethnic backgrounds. They knew the value of a strong work ethic. I learned quickly the importance of self-reliance, the intense desire and will required to get ahead and the dogged determination that would be necessary to insure success.

It wasn't uncommon to set our alarm clock at 3:00 A.M. so that I could review difficult geometry problems and other study assignments before starting the three-mile hike to school at 7:00 in the morning. I was determined to become a relatively good student and to take advantage of the education opportunities available to me.

Frequently, I found myself setting goals and challenging myself in different ways. One such goal was completing the Citizens Military Training Camp Program that was introduced to me. It consisted of thirty days of basic military training at Fort Meade, Maryland, during the summer school break each year for four consecutive years. Although the minimum age for acceptance was seventeen years, I was accepted at age fifteen—ostensibly because of my size and perceived maturity.

In June 1940 I graduated from both our Central High School and from the Citizens Military Training Camp Program. During this period Nazi Germany was running amok in Europe and wasting everything in its path. Even to us inexperienced new high school graduates, it was apparent that the United States' entry into the war in Europe was simply a matter of time.

I enlisted in the regular U.S. Army Air Corps two weeks before Pearl Harbor was bombed by the Japanese. Shortly afterwards I attended Infantry Officer's Candidate School at Fort Benning, Georgia.

Upon graduation I was commissioned a Second Lieutenant of infantry and after a brief interval found myself with the Third Infantry Division on the Anzio Beachhead in Italy. The division was heavily engaged in warding off a series of German counterattacks aimed at destroying the beachhead. I served with the Third Infantry until the war in Europe officially ended.

There is no doubt in my mind that the human qualities nurtured during my youth of self-reliance, a strong work ethic, an intense desire and will to succeed and a dogged determination to accept and successfully complete any assigned task have significantly influenced my life.

I consider these traits indispensable to my ability to survive and succeed in many small-unit combat actions on the battlefields of Europe during World War II. Further, these traits formed the underpinnings of an attitude that enabled me to pursue an enjoyable, rewarding and successful military career in the U.S. Army—for thirty-eight years.

John Tominac

Sorenson and five other Marines were in a shellhole during a two-day Japanese invasion when a grenade was thrown upon them. With no regard or second thought for his own safety, he hurled himself upon the exploding grenade ... heroically taking its full impact. Although severely wounded, he saved the lives of his comrades.

Private Richard K. Sorenson, U.S. Marine Corps Reserve
Company M, 3d Battalion, 24th Marine Regiment, 4th Marine Division
February 1–2, 1944
Namur Island, Kwajalein Atoll, Marshall Islands

Human Destiny

America has great need for young men and women
with pride in our country and faith in freedom,
unafraid to declare to anyone in the world
"I believe in liberty, I believe in justice
and will fight to defend the dignity of man."

We must dedicate ourselves to the principal
that "Freedom under God" is humanity's destiny.
We must not only live our lives according to this principal,
but also must defend it unto death
with the courage of free men.
Our great country won its freedom in one generation—
but in one generation it could also lose it.

Let us proclaim to the whole world:
"Individual freedom is our creed,
national freedom is our heritage
and world freedom is our goal."

Richard K. Sorenson

... commanding the USS Parche *against a Japanese convoy off Taiwan, Ramage launched a series of fire and torpedoes to sink the lead tanker and damage another. Soon he struck again; after ordering his men below, he remained poised alone outside the vessel in the midst of the forty-six-minute battle that ensued, which ended victoriously for Ramage and his unscathed* Parche.

Commander Lawson P. Ramage, U.S. Navy
USS *Parche*
July 31, 1944
South China Sea

Now You Know

A few years ago, I was supposed to do an interview with the oldest person I knew. The oldest person was my granddad, Vice Admiral Lawson P. Ramage. The problem was, he was back in the hospital again.

My mom told him about it, and he said he really wanted to do it. So, a couple of times, we tried having me go over to the hospital, but that didn't work out. Finally, the Thursday before Christmas, the doctor sent him home. We were all so glad to have him back home. And the day before Christmas, Granddad and I sat down at the table where he always played solitaire. He sat in his regular seat, and I sat in Grandma's seat. It was like magic. He was my old granddad all over again. Whatever I asked him, he had a quick answer. He was just like someone on television. Here are some of the things he told me.

A long time ago, when the president of the United States was Teddy Roosevelt, Granddad was born. He was the oldest of five boys. When he was nine years old, his mom died from the flu epidemic. After that, they had different housekeepers until finally his aunt came over from Scotland and brought them all up. But Granddad did lots of the bringing up too. When one of his brothers got scarlet fever, he took the others up to camp in the Adirondacks while his aunt took care of the one who was sick. His favorite time when he was a boy was when he and his brother went down to the Thousand Islands together. He told me his favorite books were *Robin Hood* and *The Deerslayer*. He liked them because they were full of action and adventure.

The chore he most remembered was digging sawdust out of the ice house and getting it prepared to store ice for the summer. He and his brothers sawed big stumps of hardwood that came down from the bowling pin factory and got good firewood. He said they were busy all the time. But Granddad was *always* busy *all the time*.

He told me his hero was Charles Lindbergh because he made the first solo flight across the Atlantic. Granddad said that what he himself really wanted was to go into the Merchant Marines. He had wanted to ever since he was five years old, when he crossed the Atlantic Ocean on a big ship. And you know, he got his wish. What he enjoyed most was the freedom of the sea. He told me that "to travel long and of your own free will is one of the most delightful things in the world."

Along the way, Granddad collected a lot of medals. He was awarded the Medal of Honor in 1945 for sinking five enemy ships by doing something that was unheard of: reloading torpedoes by hand in the midst of battle. All this took eighteen minutes but, since they figured no one would believe the truth, the official record says it took forty-six minutes.

When he died, he was the most highly decorated submariner alive.

I asked Granddad if he had any advice for kids today, and he did. He said, "Young people need to learn the price of freedom from the events going on in Europe, and how important it is to them, and how equally important it is to us to maintain our freedom and to respect the laws of this country, to refrain from drugs of all kinds and to live an upright life."

I miss my granddad. I'll always remember stroking his head when he finally stopped breathing. But most of all, I'll remember when he'd take me and my brother fishing, and when he'd take me on his lap and play computer games with me—and when he'd give me a hug and make me feel good.

This was the Granddad I knew. I think you now know him too.

Emily Laura Ramage Ross,
for her granddad,
Lawson P. Ramage

… Walsh repeatedly dove his plane into an enemy formation that outnumbered his own division six to one and, although his plane was hit numerous times, shot down two Japanese dive bombers and one fighter. Later, during a vital escort mission, he had to land his damaged craft and quickly replace it with another. Rejoining the escort group, he encountered approximately fifty Japanese Zeros. Immediately he attacked, striking fury in his lone battle against the powerful force, destroying four fighters before being forced to land in his bullet-riddled plane.

First Lieutenant Kenneth A. Walsh, U.S. Marine Corps
Marine Fighting Squadron 124, Marine Air Group 12, 1st Marine Air Wing
August 15, 30, 1943
Solomon Islands

I Remember

I just remember it was bitter cold that February morning when the limousine dropped the wife and I off at the White House. The doors to the Oval Office swung open, and there sat a sickly but grinning man—Franklin D. Roosevelt, president of the United States.

As a gaggle of admirals and generals looked on, FDR opened an oblong box on his desk with the Medal in it. I stepped up crisply and stooped as Roosevelt hung the Medal around my neck. Eyeball to eyeball, inches from the most powerful man on earth, I gulped.

"Scared, young man?" FDR asked. "Yessir!" was all I could manage.

"Lieutenant Walsh, will you shake my hand?" he asked again. "Yesssir!" was all I could say.

So, I meet the president of the United States and all I could say was "yessir"—twice.

I guess I was awed. Still am.

I joined the marines in 1933 as a private and moved up through the ranks becoming a "mustang," slang for an enlisted man who receives an officer's commission. I flew gull-winged Corsairs in the Pacific in World War II and was credited with twenty-one confirmed kills, I want you to know that I crashed or was shot down in five Corsairs. To this day some of my friends joke that I should be credited as a Japanese Ace, since I lost five of our own airplanes.

You know, I wasn't the Red Baron going off into the wild blue yonder to do battle single-handedly, as some might think. I knew the Japanese Zero, I knew how to attack it. Everything was a risk, but a calculated risk.

After the war I sought out several Japanese pilots, including one who may have shot me down. There is a camaraderie among pilots. You respect the skills of the other guy. Most have a code of ethics. I would never strafe a downed pilot. Most of them wouldn't either, though there were some isolated incidents on both sides.

The Medal has never gone to my head. I look back on everything that happened with all humility. On both the missions for which I was awarded the Medal of Honor, we lost pilots. We lost a lot of guys.

I always remember that.

In 1945, on Okinawa, I traded an infantryman a bottle of whiskey for a Japanese fighter pilot's knee message pad, which he had recovered. I kept the pad for myself as a souvenir but realized that perhaps a relative of that fighter pilot might long for such an item. The owner's name was scratched onto the clear Plexiglas backing: *Captain Sonoda*. A bloodstained note inside contained clues.

By locating Sonoda's commanding officer, Major Atsushi Yoshida, we were able to piece together his story. On a bomb run to destroy Okinawa, Captain Sonoda was shot down by antiaircraft fire and crash-landed safely. He was surrounded by our infantrymen and ordered to surrender. In response, he took out his pistol and fought it out until he was killed.

Exactly fifty years after the death of Captain Sonoda, the knee message pad was finally returned to Sonoda's nephew and to Major Atsushi Yoshida. In gratitude the major wrote:

> When I took Captain Sonoda's bloodstained board in my hands and saw the words "comradeship" that he wrote fifty years ago, and, "We were born separately but will die together," I felt as if I was brought face-to-face with him once again. My heart was filled with joy. I am at this moment looking at a photo of you, Mr. Walsh. I feel lucky not to have met you in the air fifty years ago in the skies over Okinawa. I would feel even more lucky if I were able to meet you someday.

Ken Walsh
Lieutenant Colonel, USMC (Retired)

… when his roadblock was about to be overrun by attacking enemy tanks, Vlug left his position and with a rocket launcher single-handedly destroyed tank after tank, flanking them and eliminating them despite a hail of enemy fire.

Private First Class Dirk J. Vlug, U.S. Army
Headquarters Company, 1st Battalion, 126th Infantry, 32d Infantry Division
December 15, 1944
Near Limon, Leyte, Philippine Islands

Birds

During my boyhood days, I lived in the country
and liked watching the animals and birds.
I especially liked the birds and learned much from them.
They could always fend for themselves
and could adapt to any situation.

At about twelve years of age, I built my first birdhouse.

After I retired I again spent much of my time
building birdhouses and feeders,
and giving them to neighbors and friends—
and putting blue birdhouses along the highway.

I've said my retirement was for "The Birds."
I believe we can learn how to cope with a lot in life
by watching them.

Dirk Vlug

… Oresko moved alone toward deadly enemy fire, threw a grenade at a bunker and followed it up with point-blank rifle fire, eliminating all inside. Bleeding from a hip wound, he refused to be evacuated but continued to move on, assaulting more and more enemy troops manning machine-gun positions until defeating them.

Master Sergeant Nicholas Oresko, U.S. Army
Company C, 302d Infantry, 94th Infantry Division
January 23, 1945
Near Tettington, Germany

How Lucky Can One Be?

As a young boy, whenever I felt tired or slightly ill, my dear mother would encourage me to keep going. She would say, "Don't give in to yourself, keep going and doing; you can always do more than you realize. It's just too easy to quit."

To this day my grown son continues to thank me for instilling this same philosophy in him.

In life we come upon many obstacles. It amazes me how one steady individual can have a calming influence on others nearby.

It is difficult to say who the person is behind the Medal. In life, as in war, no one knows what he or she is capable of doing at a given moment. You rise to the occasion.

No matter how firm your plans may be, unknown forces out there will somehow affect your best laid plans. One must be flexible.

My wife and I eloped during the early part of World War II. It was a honeymoon for almost forty years before she died. It was so because we both continually worked at it. She died fifteen years ago, and I was alone—alone. Later I met a lonely lady at a widowed group, and life is good again. Again I have a friend who helps and listens.

Again it works because we both work at it. How lucky can one be!

Nicholas Oresko

… just after "Bombs Away," the plane Pucket was piloting received heavy antiaircraft fire, killing one and severely wounding six others. With the aircraft crippled, Pucket turned the controls over to his copilot while he calmed his crew, administered first aid and surveyed the options. Realizing they were losing altitude, he ordered the crew to abandon ship … all but three left the plane. He urged the others to jump, but they refused. He wouldn't abandon the three hysterical men and was last seen fighting to regain control of the plane as it crashed into a mountainside.

First Lieutenant Donald D. Pucket, U.S. Army Air Corps
343d Bombardment Squadron, 98th Bombardment Group, 8th Air Force
July 9, 1944
Ploesti, Romania

Flying and the Captain of the Ship

Don loved to fly
and was an avid skier: we were few in 1940.
He always said skiing
was the next best thing to flying.

Don's action in staying with his wounded crewmembers
and crippled B-24 was what was
"traditional and expected of the Captain of the Ship."

Lorene Vervalin,
remembering her husband,
Don D. Pucket

With his company pinned down by German fire, Ogden advanced alone, armed with various weapons, up a slope toward enemy emplacements. Wounded by a machine-gun bullet, he managed to reach a vantage point, from where he was able to silence most of the German weapons that had plagued his unit as they guarded the approach to Cherbourg, France.

**First Lieutenant Carlos C. Ogden, Sr., U.S. Army
Company K, 314th Infantry, 79th Infantry Division
June 25, 1944
Near Fort du Roule, France**

Family—and the Glue That Binds

When it is all said and done, family is the most important segment of our lives.

I must say that my mother was a wonderful lady, the "glue" that kept our family together during the difficult depression years. I had great love and respect for her.

She loved me and was always there for me in spite of the times I disappointed her—which were many. She was proud of my accomplishments, always.

After I left the army and the wartime experiences were behind me, I was determined to devote as much of my time as possible to my family. Part of this determination was due to the fact that my father never spent time with me as I was growing up.

Fortunately, I was able to spend more time with our four boys than most fathers do. I enjoyed this thoroughly, and I think they did too. We had lots of fun.

We did all the "boy things," from Cub Scouts to Boy Scouts, Little League, Pony League and American Legion League Baseball and basketball in the driveway. Two of the boys became all-Americans in basketball, one in high school and the other in college. We had an all-American swimmer and a high school high jumper.

When I look back, the memories are priceless.

And yes, kudos must go to my wife of fifty-three years, Louise, who in our family has been the "glue" holding it all together.

Carlos C. Ogden

... over a four-month period, Bulkeley led his men in missions to damage or destroy numerous enemy planes and ships, in addition to dispersing countless landing parties and land-based forces, using brilliant skills, unique resourcefulness and ingenuity. So unprecedented were the actions of his men and himself that films and books have vividly portrayed these events.

Lieutenant Commander John Duncan Bulkeley, U.S. Navy
Motor Torpedo Boat Squadron 3
December 7, 1941–April 10, 1942
Philippine Waters

Genuine Satisfaction

The greatest satisfaction of any human being
is to be able to be satisfied in what he has done with his life,
that he is proud of it.

Yes, you get medals and can be awarded all this recognition,
but that is kind of hollow.

If you are satisfied with yourself, and in whatever job you have,
that is the greatest satisfaction you can have
and no one can take that away from you.

John D. Bulkeley
Vice Admiral, USN

… Wetzel was a door-gunner on a helicopter trapped in a landing zone when his commander was wounded. Without hesitation, he went to the commander's aid, but a blast threw him into a rice paddy. He suffered multiple wounds, including a lost left arm. As enemy fire intensified, Wetzel staggered back to his machine gun and eliminated the enemy emplacement. In and out of consciousness, he continued to provide aid to his crew and commander.

Private First Class Gary G. Wetzel, U.S. Army
173d Assault Helicopter Company, 1st Aviation Brigade
January 8, 1968
Near Ap Dong An, Vietnam

Sacrifices Yesterday and Today

I really believe in our Constitution where it starts out "We the People." That means you and me. We are brought up in a society where we are born into FREE-DOM—a gift I deeply cherish. And I also understand the sacrifices men and women of yesterday have made for me.

When I speak to students, I try to talk about today and tomorrow, of all the wonderful things that we can look forward to, things we take for granted, electricity, ice cream and the right to express one's opinion openly and freely without getting arrested. I also remind them about the sacrifices of our forefathers.

Then I talk about unity and the accomplishments that we have made and we can make if we put our thoughts and ideas together.

When speaking, I reach into my pocket and pull my hand out and wave it out at the crowd. They look bewildered at what I'm doing, but I continue to speak. When I start talking about unity and accomplishments as a group, I finally tell them I was passing grains of salt that no one could see at that moment. Pulling out the plastic bag of salt from my pocket I say that when we unite and work together, this is what we can accomplish.

Remember that throughout life, to get anything accomplished, we all at one time or another have to make personal sacrifices.

Gary Wetzel

After a month of fighting at the Munda Airstrip, Scott pushed forward alone and when encountering a Japanese attack, gained possession of a hill. With only a tree stump for cover, he stood his ground against them and threw grenades with uncanny accuracy, even though he had a bullet wound in his hand and shrapnel in his head. Eventually, American troops swept across the plateau to conquer the hill and four days later, capture the airstrip.

Second Lieutenant Robert S. Scott, U.S. Army
Company C, 1st Battalion, 172d Infantry, 43d Infantry Division
July 29, 1943
New Georgia, Solomon Islands

Henceforth Duty and Honor Bound

At Garfield Junior High School in Berkeley, California, I was a student in a civics class in 1927. I was fourteen years old then, and I've forgotten the teacher's name, but I've never forgotten the lesson he taught me.

Each student in the class was to write a report of a daylong field trip we had taken to various offices of the city government of Berkeley and the county government of Contra Costa County.

A best friend had written a well-organized report. I rationalized that since I had taken the same trip, had observed the same governmental functions and had shared his observations and opinions, it would be simple to use his report, paraphrase his vocabulary and submit his work as my own. So that's what I did.

Some weeks later the teacher called me and my friend to his desk in front of the entire class, handed each of us his report, and asked, "which of these two reports is the original?" I immediately and truthfully acknowledged that my friend's report was the original. But, I was embarrassed and ashamed in the presence of my whole class.

Since then, I've flunked university classes for failing to withdraw within the time constraints, or failing to attend class, but never for cheating or submitting anyone else's work as my own. My attitude hasn't been correct some of the time, but it has been my own. I've long since concluded that I would have benefited more from my formal education had several more teachers or professors cared enough about my work to call me in and give me a critical evaluation of my failure to perform up to capabilities—in other words, to give me a good "chewing out."

I was awarded the Medal of Honor in World War II for deeds one day as a Second Lieutenant infantry platoon leader, deeds that I initiated at least in part from the conviction that I ought to have enough guts to do what I was authorized to order a sergeant or private soldier to try to do. And I wanted the enlisted men and the officers to respect me and to judge me a man.

In 1945 at Fort Benning, Georgia, a World War I Medal of Honor recipient, Colonel Sam Parker, verbally informed me that I was henceforth duty and honor bound to conduct myself so as never to reflect dishonor or disgrace on the Congressional Medal of Honor.

I've never forgotten that, either!

Bob Scott

… flying on a mission to rescue a small special forces group near Duc Co, Fleming attempted to land unsuccessfully once, knowing the helicopter before him didn't make it. Low on fuel, his only choice to repeat his first landing maneuver, his aircraft remained in an exposed position. The second time, he landed on target, and the stranded patrol boarded the helicopter. With a barrage of hostile fire crashing through the window and around his craft, he made a successful takeoff and finally landed safely at a forward base.

First Lieutenant James P. Fleming, U.S. Air Force
20th Special Operations Squadron
November 26, 1968
Near Duc Co, Vietnam

No More, No Less

I had the high honor and privilege
of being a helicopter pilot in the Vietnam War.

It was my mission
to insert and extract American and allied soldiers in combat.

I did what every other helicopter pilot did:
no more, no less.

What is different about me is that
I was awarded the Medal of Honor.

Therefore, it's my honor, privilege and duty
to represent those who served as helicopter pilots
during the Vietnam War.

James P. Fleming

While on a bombing mission to Germany, Michael's B-17 aircraft was singled out and attacked by a swarm of enemy fighters. The plane was riddled from nose to tail from cannon shells, including one that exploded in the cockpit, injuring both pilots. With the bomb bay in flames and the plane going down, Michael ordered the crew to bail out—seven did, but the bombardier stayed aboard, because his parachute was inoperable. Michael's only choice was to fly the plane until he became exhausted from blood loss, at which point his copilot took the controls. Regaining consciousness, he landed the severely crippled plane on the English coast, saving the lives of the remaining crew.

**First Lieutenant Edward S. Michael, U.S. Army Air Corps/U.S. Air Force
364th Bombardment Squadron, 2d Air Division, 8th Air Force
April 11, 1944
Stettin, Germany**

The Greatest Heritage

Shortly after my husband passed away in 1994, I was leafing through his scriptures one day when I ran across a faded sheet of yellow notebook paper with his writing on it. It was dated June 25, 1966. It is but a tiny drop of the true essence of my late husband.

To My Future Americans,

You, as an American, as your forefathers before you, know that our flag is the one true symbol of freedom that is accepted by most people of the world.

That this image we see of ourselves in the eyes, and can feel in the hearts of people of suppressed nations, did not come about without much sacrifice. Much blood was spilled for you and I over and over again, so that we could remain free.

Freedom, my greatest heritage, I bequeath to you. Honor it with your life—for without it, what good is life?

Edward S. Michael
An American

Louise E. Michael,
remembering
Edward S. Michael

… when all of his superior officers were either killed or wounded, Schonland valiantly continued fighting to free the USS San Francisco *of large quantities of water flooding the second deck through numerous shellholes caused by enemy fire. Being told he was now commanding officer, Schonland chose to continue resuming the vital work of maintaining the ship's stability. In water waist deep, he labored in darkness, illuminated only by hand lanterns, until he had drained enough water from the flooded compartments to restore the ship and limp it back to port under its own power.*

Commander Herbert E. Schonland, U.S. Navy
USS *San Francisco*
November 12–13, 1943
Iron Bottom Sound, Solomon Islands

The Nobility of It

The following reflects the thinking of my late husband, Rear Admiral Herbert E. Schonland, on a critical wartime skill, damage control. He left this as one of his many contributions to the United States Naval Officers Damage Control School:

> *You can't think twice when you have damage.*
> *That's why war is for youth. Older men stop and think twice. That's fatal.*
> *The young don't stop to think. They act instinctively.*
> *In damage control if you've made an error, it's too late. You can't retrace your steps.*

In this message, you find both the nobility of the man and a little bit of his humor and irony.

For even as he exhorted the next generation of seamen with these words, he was actually passing to them the torch of leadership. Have the confidence to act; be bold, he was telling them.

In combat he knew you couldn't afford to merely let those older or higher in rank make all the decisions. Though that might be comfortable, it costs precious time and too often, precious lives.

Claire M. Schonland,
remembering her husband,
Herbert E. Schonland

... during Operation Hastings, Modrzejewski's company successfully seized a large supply area, setting the stage for a two-and-a-half-day battle. In the first series of attacks, his unit repulsed an overwhelming assault, only to face a battalion-size enemy element the following night. During this second attack, Modrzejewski's unit was surrounded, and he was seriously wounded, yet he crawled more than two hundred meters to deliver essential ammunition to his exposed men and directed artillery fire to within a few meters of his position to ward off the enemy. The third day, additional enemy moved in, and although now vastly outnumbered, he led his men to boldly halt the assault.

Captain Robert J. Modrzejewski, U.S. Marine Corps
Company K, 3d Battalion, 4th Marines, 3d Marine Division
July 15–18, 1966
Republic of Vietnam

Get the Priorities in Order

For many years my religious beliefs were superficial.
I became used to thinking about everything
except the good Lord
and what He had given me.
I don't think I ever thanked Him for anything.

After a very serious medical operation,
my relationship with God changed completely.
No longer did pride prevent me from becoming closer to Him.

Since that time I've tried to give something back
to my church and community.
My life is now God, Family and Country—
but it took a crisis for me to get my priorities in order.

Robert J. Modrzejewski

... with his copilot killed, eight crewmembers wounded, one engine on fire and no visible controls, pilot Lawley elected to remain in control of his B-17. Enemy fighters again attacked, but by using masterful evasive actions, he managed to lose them. After being seriously wounded, he collapsed, was revived by a crewman and kept control of the aircraft until he made a successful crash landing off the English coast.

First Lieutenant William R. Lawley, Jr., U.S. Army Air Corps/U.S. Air Force
364th Bombardment Squadron, 305th Bombardment Group, 8th Air Force
February 20, 1944
Over Europe

A Most Rewarding and Fulfilling Life

I was born in Leeds, Alabama, a small Alabama town, back in 1920. Now the town is almost a continuation of Birmingham. Basically it is a coal-mining and small-business community of hardworking, religious and family-conscious people.

I was an only child by a father whose first wife had died and who then married my mother. I had six half brothers and sisters, some still at home when my father married my mother, and we had a very happy and normal life. I grew up playing ball, hunting, fishing and taking advantage of all the good things a small town had to offer in the "olden days."

I graduated from high school but had no opportunity to attend college. So I went to work driving a Coca-Cola delivery truck and later opened my own small filling station in Birmingham. I was running this filling station in 1941 during the attack on Pearl Harbor, and I knew that I wanted to enlist and be a pilot. I had no desire to be in the army as such and thought this would be my best opportunity. I was accepted in the Aviation Cadet program and graduated in the pilot class of 43-D.

The day before my graduation I married Amelia Dodd of Denison, Texas, whom I had met while a cadet at Perrin Field, Texas. As of this date, October 24, 1995, we have been married fifty-two years and have three children, two girls and a boy, plus four grandchildren.

I stayed in the air force after the war and retired in September 1972 in the rank of colonel. I enjoyed my air force service and the many interesting assignments, including Assistant Air Attache at our embassy in Brazil, and Defense and Air Attache at our embassy in Manila, Republic of the Philippines.

Since retiring, I have served with a Good Roads Citizens Group and as executive director of the Alabama Asphalt Pavement Association for a short time.

We have a lake cottage—my pride and joy—and I enjoy every minute spent there. All our children are great boating and skiing enthusiasts, and when they return home, the lake is where we congregate and have wonderful times.

I'm still invited to speak at the Air University schools at Maxwell Air Force Base in Alabama and, as all recipients of the Medal of Honor do, I speak at schools and civic clubs.

As most of my generation are, I'm terribly disturbed by the number of illegitimate births today, the use of drugs and the violent crime so prevalent everywhere in our country. I stress the need for more morality whenever given a chance.

My entire life has been devoted to being the best air force officer I could be. I feel I have had a most rewarding and fulfilling life with my experiences, my family and my many, many friends.

William R. Lawley, Jr.

… leading his battalion along eight miles of primitive icy trails in the bitter cold to relieve a rifle company and seize control of a vital mountain pass, Davis constantly remained in the thick of the fighting as he climbed over three ridges. Although knocked down and wounded, he arose to lead his men to the isolated marines and secure the pass from a strongly entrenched Korean enemy. Despite repeated assaults, the battalion held the vital terrain, allowing two marine regiments to deploy through the area.

Lieutenant Colonel Raymond G. Davis, U.S. Marine Corps
1st Battalion, 7th Marines, 1st Marine Division
December 1–4, 1950
Hagaru-ri, Korea

My Honor, Their Devotion

The Medal of Honor is an ever-present challenge
to the wearer to be worthy of it.

I wear the "Medal" in honor and memory
of those gallant warriors
whose superb performance
gained success in our challenging efforts.

It was their peerless devotion
and dedication to the battle tasks,
their all for one and one for all spirit,
which made my leadership effective.

As it is in most combat successes,
teamwork was the key.

From the heart,
General Raymond G. Davis

... Drowley refused to remain under cover, instead fearlessly rushing to aid wounded soldiers. During this rescue, he mounted an American tank and directed it toward an enemy pillbox that was causing heavy casualties. Not only did he silence the intended pillbox, but also he destroyed another alongside it, even though he had severe bullet wounds to the chest and left eye.

Staff Sergeant Jesse R. Drowley, U.S. Army
Company B, 1st Battalion, 132d Infantry, Americal Division
January 30, 1944
Bougainville, Solomon Islands

OK, Let's Go

When I was growing up in northern Michigan, being the oldest son, my father expected a lot of me. I never liked to disappoint him.

He built log homes and lodges in resort areas near the lakes. We cut and hauled pulp many miles to the mill. Finally we had a sawmill and cut and sawed lumber until I left for the army in April 1941.

It was hard work and long hours, with many difficult jobs to do. Dad always figured there was a way to accomplish almost anything; you just had to figure out how. If you did it right the first time, you wouldn't need to do it over!

If it was a bulldozer or "Cat" that had broken down and you had to figure how to get a big nonrunning piece of machinery loaded onto a truck or trailer to take home to repair, or how to load the trucks so you did not have your load shift or lose it on a curve, it was always a challenge.

We would try different methods until we found a system that worked, and there was always a good feeling of satisfaction when you accomplished it, and Dad would say, "OK, let's go." He would not say much more if he was pleased, but you did know it if he wasn't!

I learned from him about responsibility and doing the job right. I think it builds up your confidence in yourself to know you can handle a difficult task. It has always given me a sense of satisfaction knowing I could rely on myself and meet a challenge.

Jesse Drowley

… although devastated by cannon fire, the captain rallied his men and led them up a steep coral hill to the summit in the midst of vicious enemy fire. Limited on weapons, ammunition and water, Pope remained on the exposed hill with twelve soldiers and one wounded officer. Although continuously attacked, they endured through the night.

Captain Everett P. Pope, U.S. Marine Corps
Company C, 1st Battalion, 1st Marines, 1st Marine Division
September 19–20, 1944
Peleliu Island, Palau Islands

The Citizen-Soldier

As the years have passed, I have become quite friendly with a distinguished gentleman named Joshua Lawrence Chamberlain. Now you may say that since he served in the Civil War, and I in World War II, such a friendship is highly unlikely, if not impossible.

Let me explain.

Lawrence, as he was widely known, graduated in 1852 from my alma mater, Bowdoin College, which was then, as it is today, a small, distinguished liberal arts college on the coast of Maine. He was serving on the college's faculty in 1861 when he volunteered for service in the Union Army.

His career is legend: dozens of major engagements and many wounds. His best known action, of course, was at Gettysburg, where he and his 20th Maine Regiment defended Little Round Top. He prevented the left flank of the Union army from being turned, an action for which he received the Medal of Honor.

Promoted by Grant to Brevet Major General, he was chosen to receive the surrender of Lee's army at Appomatox Court House. He returned to Maine, served four terms as governor, and then for ten years was president of Bowdoin College.

I was privileged to be that Bowdoin graduate next after Chamberlain to receive a Medal of Honor. I also was honored to serve Bowdoin, not as its president but as Chairman of its Board of Trustees—so I have always found a kinship of interest with Lawrence!

My admiration for Chamberlain lies in the fact that he was the absolute epitome of the citizen-soldier: taking up arms when his country called and returning to his civilian career when victory was won.

In that sense my military career followed in his tracks. I entered the Marine Corps four days after graduating from Bowdoin in 1941, served voluntarily (as did millions of others) until the end of the war and returned to civilian life.

Our nation depends on the citizen-soldier, as it has since the battle of Lexington in 1775.

So Joshua Lawrence Chamberlain and I are good friends—although a century of history divides our lives. His was a life that any one of us would be proud to emulate.

Everett P. Pope

... with the Germans awaiting in three echelons—at fifty, one hundred and three hundred yards away—the platoon leader fired his rifle and three grenades, disabling the first group at fifty yards. Montgomery then called for an artillery attack on the second group, and armed with a carbine, attacked the position himself until seven enemies surrendered to him. Continuing on to the last position, when the artillery barrage lifted, he ran fearlessly toward where the surrendering Germans started streaming out of their position to face him.

First Lieutenant Jack C. Montgomery, U.S. Army
Company 1, 3d Battalion, 180th Infantry, 45th Infantry Division
February 22, 1944
Near Padiglione, Italy

Love of Country

My hope, my country
in her dealings with other countries,
may she always be right.

But, right or wrong,
she's still my country.

Jack C. Montgomery

… acting as platoon leader during intense Japanese gunfire, Rudolph led the attack by individually charging machine-gun and rifle pillboxes and dropping in grenades. He single-handedly neutralized a total of eight enemy emplacements. Later, when his platoon was attacked by an enemy tank, he rushed it, climbed on top and dropped a grenade in the turret to destroy the crew.

Technical Sergeant Donald E. Rudolph, U.S. Army
Company E, 20th Infantry, 6th Infantry Division
February 5, 1945
Munoz, Luzon, Philippine Islands

A Summer on the Road

In June 1940 I graduated from North High School, Minneapolis, Minnesota.

Having planned the general scheme of travel with a friend of mine, we left Minneapolis, hitchhiking to Chelan, Washington. He was going to enter the CCC; I was trying to find some kind of summer work. Our second ride dropped us off on the flats in South Dakota. After a lot of walking to get to a lone tree for some shade, a car pulling another car picked us up. They were going to Seattle, Washington. Even though they weren't allowed to pick up riders, they did—of course, they caught heck the next day for taking us along. When two drivers left the caravan, my friend and I were given cars to drive—and the man in charge was glad to have us driving for him.

We completed the driving at Wenatchee to head north to Chelan.

My friend got back into the CCC, and I first got a job in an apple orchard thinning apples, then other jobs that got me through until the time for picking. I earned four cents a box. I picked 150 boxes and paid one dollar for room and board.

When the harvest was over, I had one hundred dollars in my pocket and started back to Minnesota. I got a ride to Spokane, Washington, then another to Coeur d'Alene. I had a noon lunch for fifty cents and gave the waitress a ten dollar bill. She gave me nine silver dollars. They didn't have paper dollars, and I sure wish I'd saved the silver!

I had Minneapolis, Minnesota, on the side of my travel bag. I noticed the driver of a Durant automobile go by me first one direction, then the other. Then it made another U-turn and stopped. The driver, his wife and one daughter were going through Minneapolis into Wisconsin.

They were not planning to pick up a hitchhiker. They thought I was dressed cleanly and picked me up. I let them know I had a driver's license.

Going through Montana the first night, the car's generator burned out. The moon was out at full light so I suggested I drive by moonlight and turn the park lights on when a car passed or approached us. I drove as far as we could and found a secondhand shop and a motel. I said I would sleep out in the car, but they insisted I sleep inside the motel.

In the morning they took out the generator and exchanged it for a repaired one. We got in and were on the road again. The driver informed me that he had a gas station in Seattle—and that he'd give a job if I ever got there.

We drove the last day until that moment when I pulled over to the curb. Giving them my thanks, I walked the half block to home. I had given them information to get to Highway 12, going east toward their destination.

Yes, I remember hitchhiking from Chelan to Minneapolis and back again. Those were the days: "three cars" each way, and a pretty good distance.

The trip served me well during the coming war years.

Donald E. Rudolph

... as the company commander, Bucha and his unit were dropped into an enemy stronghold and attacked by enemy armed with automatic weapons, rockets and grenades. Pinned down by a machine-gun bunker, he crawled through a hail of fire to destroy the bunker. Outnumbered four to one by the charging enemy, he ordered and covered a withdrawal but was ambushed once again. He ordered his men to play dead while he called in artillery fire around them. Then throughout the night he moved from position to position, encouraging his men.

Captain Paul W. Bucha, U.S. Army
Company D, 3d Battalion, 187th Infantry, 101st Airborne Division
March 16–19, 1968
Near Phuoc Vinh, Binh Duong Province, Vietnam

Who'll Tell Them?

The Medal of Honor is a collection of people;
their stories, their descriptions and their personal feelings.

Third parties can't convey it.
Many films—and many people—have tried
to portray Medal of Honor recipients
and their innermost selves.

They always fail.

Every recipient I've met has had a very human story to tell.
There will come a time when the men are gone.

When they're gone, who's going to tell their story?
Who's going to tell the young people that come
after us that we're all human, that compassion,
professionalism and pride are what's important—
not charging up and down hills.

Paul W. Bucha

... on a volunteer rescue mission, Pilot Jackson defied all odds by deciding to try landing his aircraft in an attempt to rescue a three-man Combat Control Team. Incredibly, he landed his plane near the beleaguered men, immediately becoming the target of intense hostile fire. With those rescued on board, he miraculously was able to lift off and head to safety.

Lieutenant Colonel Joe M. Jackson, U.S. Air Force
311th Air Commando Squadron
May 12, 1968
Kham Duc, Vietnam

Do What's Right

When I was a young boy about the age of twelve, I became a Christian.

One of the things my mother and my minister taught me was to always do the right thing. This is spelled out in the Bible in the fourth chapter of John, verse seventeen. I've tried to live up to this requirement, not always being successful—but I've always tried.

The right thing may not be what you as an individual would like, but if it is the right thing, then do it. Major decisions become a lot easier when the right thing is used as a benchmark.

As I grew older, I began to establish goals for myself and to plot the milestones necessary to achieve those goals. Once you do this, don't ever lose sight of the goals. Focus everything in the direction of those goals.

Above all, never give up!

And remember, people are never a failure until they quit trying.

Joe M. Jackson

The corporal jumped from his shelter, wielding a bayonet to eliminate ten enemy soldiers in close combat. As Miyamura gave first aid to his fellow soldiers, another assault hit his area. He manned his machine gun until there was no more ammunition and ordered his squad to withdraw, while he stayed behind and bayoneted his way through until the attack became too intense. Before his position was overrun, he alone, although severely wounded, was responsible for eliminating more than fifty attackers.

Corporal Hiroshi H. Miyamura, U.S. Army
Company H, 7th Infantry Regiment, 3d Infantry Division
April 24–25, 1951
Near Taejon-ni, Korea

He Will Not Let You Down

I would like to share with you my thoughts
and beliefs while growing up and the same thoughts
and beliefs I try to live by today.

I am most grateful to my parents
for making me attend Sunday school as a youngster.
I found out early in life that there is a God
and He has certain rules we have to live by;
and we should always have faith in Him.
I believe if we have faith in God and live by His rules,
He will not let you down.

That same faith is what made this country
the greatest country in all the world.

Hiroshi Miyamura

Stopped by heavy German fire on Monticelli Ridge, Johnson held an exposed position alone for three days, after his entire squad was either killed or wounded. With grenades and small-arms fire, he repulsed their attack, protecting his company's exposed left flank; he remained awake and alert, stopping all enemy attempts at infiltration until twenty-five Germans surrendered to him and twenty lay dead in front of his position. Only then did he rush to give cover and medical aid to two fellow soldiers, who lay half buried in a shellhole.

Private First Class Oscar G. Johnson, Jr., U.S. Army
Company B, 363d Infantry, 91st Infantry Division
September 16–18, 1944
Near Scarperia, Italy

What It Means to Me

Having the Medal of Honor has meant a lot to me, although it's hard to live up to it. I don't want anything to tarnish or hurt the Medal's reputation, so I must always watch what I do or say, requiring me to live at a higher level than most.

My first and second wife both made many friends at the Congressional Medal of Honor Society biannual meetings and had such good times at the Presidential Inaugurations and at the Welcome Home Celebration in New York City.

I also have been able to meet people who were with our 91st Division in both world wars. Mr. Katz from World War I was in C Company 363, while I was in B Company 363 in World War II. I met Stanley Adams who was in Italy with F Company 363 during World War II and positioned just down the line from me. He received his Medal for action in Korea.

When I was about ten years old, I read magazines that were about World War I aviators. I read lots about Eddie Rickenbacker, the renowned ace pilot and Medal of Honor recipient. I tried to follow everything he did. He was one of my favorite people. At a meeting in Florida, I got a chance to shake hands and talk with him, so I told about reading of him many years before. He died less than a year later.

I am a part-time farmer and served full-time in the Michigan National Guard from 1950 to 1980, climbing the ranks from Corporal to Chief Warrant Officer Four. Young people in the National Guard always asked many questions about World War II and what it was really like—at least as I saw it. I think I helped them by answering honestly.

Oscar G. Johnson

... after being held up for two days by a Japanese force near Cognon, Nett spearheaded an assault with another unit against the enemy as they fought from positions around a three-story building. He personally eliminated seven Japanese with his rifle and bayonet, and although wounded, he was unwilling to stop and pressed ahead with his troops to assure capture of the objective.

First Lieutenant Robert B. Nett, U.S. Army
Company E, 305th Infantry, 77th Infantry Division
December 14, 1944
Near Cognon, Leyte, Philippine Islands

A Proud Heritage

Having taught fifteen years in the Muscogee County school system, I have had the opportunity to meet thousands of young people of this era. If I were to express my one most important thought, it would be the deep appreciation I have for the wars that the citizens of this great country have participated in. And certainly World War II stands foremost in my mind.

During World War II, the United States became a totally united country, to include the civilian population. To accomplish such a total victory, after only four-and-a-half short years, is just unbelievable to me; and I feel very strongly that the students of today should be made aware of these achievements and walk proud in the light of what their fathers, grandfathers and great-grandfathers have accomplished.

The World War II victory of yesteryear is just one key to the door of freedom, so that we all can be free here today.

I want students to know that education is an essential element in them becoming good citizens. Abraham Lincoln said, "A country with no regard for its past will do little worth remembering in the future." In addition to education, they must also learn to appreciate others and the view of others. And, along with these, achieve an appreciation for the property of others.

The youth of today is the strength of tomorrow. And each of us is responsible to ensure that property is not misused or unnecessarily damaged. It is my hope that the youth of today will be strong enough to take those that violate this principle to task.

Make your fellow citizens take responsibility for their actions. We all need to realize that we rely upon each other to be successful as a nation. Individuals can not go on by themselves without considering that their fellow Americans are also striving to do the best they can with what they have. Whatever we have, we must care for it properly and use it to the maximum potential.

As I was presented the Medal of Honor, I remember accepting it not only for myself, but for all those soldiers under my command that 14th day of December 1944. I have the Medal of Honor with all the courageous soldiers in E Company, 305th Infantry, 77th Division.

It was the continuous support they gave me, both during our training phase and in those successful combat missions, which made this medal possible. Therefore, I share both the honor and glory of the Medal with all of those courageous soldiers of E Company.

Often, I am referred to as a "hero," but those soldiers were the true heroes that day. Perhaps this will help you to decide in your own mind what really makes a hero.

Please always remember, quoting General George S. Patton, that "Wars may be fought with weapons, but they are won by men. It is the spirit of the man who follows and of the man who leads that gains victory."

Robert Nett

... McCarthy fearlessly led the way across fire-swept ground, charged a pillbox and hurled hand grenades into the enemy area. He eliminated two Japanese soldiers attempting an escape. Soon after, finding another soldier attempting to kill an American, he jumped, disarmed and shot the Japanese, then rallied the remainder of his rifle company to press a full attack and capture the ridge approaching Motoyama Airfield #2.

Captain Joseph J. McCarthy, U.S. Marine Corps Reserve
Company G, 2d Battalion, 24th Marines, 4th Marine Division
February 21, 1945
Iwo Jima, Volcano Islands

Still, I Can See Them

I went in the marines a First Sergeant
and came out a Captain.

The day we landed on Iwo Jima,
I had 254 men and 7 officers in my company.
Only 12 survived.

I had a stroke a few months ago,
and I have a little trouble talking and writing sometimes,
but I don't have any trouble remembering all my boys.
I can still see their faces, all those brave boys.

Doesn't matter how many years go by,
I can see them—
and I know what they gave for this country.
I loved them all!

Joseph McCarthy

Novosel flew a medical evacuation helicopter into a heavily fortified enemy training area to rescue friendly Vietnamese soldiers. Flying with no air support, no cover and no communications with the troops down below, he maneuvered through fifteen extremely hazardous missions, under continuous fire and flying dangerously low to the ground, until all personnel were removed. He saved the lives of twenty-nine soldiers.

Chief Warrant Officer Michael J. Novosel, U.S. Army
82d Medical Detachment, 45th Medical Company, 68th Medical Group
October 2, 1969
Kien Tuong Province, Vietnam

The Dedication of the "Dustoff" Crews

I was a happily married individual with a beautiful wife and four wonderful children. At forty-seven years of age, I had been a military pilot for twenty-seven years and should have been considering retirement. After all, I had seen combat in World War II as a B-29 aircraft commander in the air offensive against Japan. I served again during the Korean War but had not been given a combat assignment.

In late 1969 I was in Vietnam on my second tour of combat there. My health was excellent except that I was taking daily medication to counter the effects of glaucoma, a serious eye disease. I was flying as a medical evacuation helicopter pilot. In the army aviation community we were known as "Dustoff Pilots," the designation and call sign of those helicopter pilots dedicated to the mission of rescuing wounded from the battle scene.

On October 2, 1969, I found myself in a battle for my life, for the lives of my crewmen, and for the lives of an undetermined number of South Vietnamese soldiers. During two-and-a-half harrowing hours, my crew and I were able to rescue twenty-nine wounded troopers. Most were severely wounded, but all survived. I was wounded during the engagement, and the helicopter was riddled by enemy fire, but we were able to return to base before the end of the day. We had flown eleven hours that day and had been on continuous duty for twenty.

The Medal of Honor was presented to me for that rescue, just one of 2,543 missions that I had flown in my two tours of duty in Vietnam. To me that mission was typical of most rescue attempts that I and all of my "Dustoff" associates had performed. Still, I cannot say enough about the actions of my crew, who never flinched in the performance of their duties, and whose lives were in jeopardy as much as mine. Their spirited dedication to the task at hand, their tireless efforts on behalf of our allied soldiers typified the work of "Dustoff" crews throughout that long and tortuous war.

Michael J. Novosel

As company commander, Schowalter was trying to attack and occupy an enemy position when one of his platoons suffered massive casualties under close enemy fire. He continued the assault, led his men into the trenches and began pounding the enemy from bunkers. Wounded again and yet again, the lieutenant wouldn't give up command and continued issuing orders and encouraging his men until their ground was secured and he could be evacuated.

**First Lieutenant Edward R. Schowalter, Jr., U.S. Army
Company A, 31st Infantry Regiment, 7th Infantry Division
October 14, 1952
Near Kumhwa, Korea**

How Do You Feel?

After the Korean War, I was going through Airborne School in the 11th Airborne Division. I was to receive command of a company upon graduation.

My battalion commander came into the sheds where we were in "hanging agony." This is where you are dangling in your parachute harness practicing pulling on your risers so as to slip to the right or left. Unfortunately the rafters of the shed to which the lines were fixed did not give like a parachute in the air, so after ten minutes you felt like you were being cut in half. The battalion commander asked how I was doing. I replied, "It hurts." He left.

At the end of the day, an airborne instructor told me that my commander wanted to see me. I reported in to him. He kept me standing at attention and said, "Mister, you are a regular army officer and soon to be a paratrooper. I don't care if you're bleeding to death—when someone asks you how you feel, you respond *Great!*"

Edward R. Schowalter, Jr.

… armed with only pistols, Maxwell and three other soldiers defended their post against an overwhelming enemy supported with superior fire. When a grenade was thrown into his squad, he hurled himself upon it … absorbing the explosion's full force. Though permanently maimed, he selflessly saved the lives of his comrades.

Technician Fifth Grade Robert D. Maxwell, U.S. Army
Headquarters Company, 7th Infantry Regiment, 3rd Infantry Division
September 7, 1944
Near Besancon, France

He Has a Future for You

Before the war I dreamed of becoming a military aviator,
but when the time came for me to respond to a call
for military service,
I chickened out and waited to be drafted.

I did not have a great fear of war,
but placed myself in the hands of my superiors,
and most of all, trusted in God.
I encountered many extremely frightening instances,
as do all front line soldiers.
I believe that when you are in God's care,
and He has a future for you,
you can survive any traumatic experience—
providing, of course, you try to follow the rules
of the Bible and trust your soul
to the saving power of Jesus.

Bob Maxwell

… along the German Anzio-Netuno defense line, Newman and four scouts were suddenly fired upon. He remained standing, found enemy nests and called back orders to his platoon. The squad was pinned down, so he advanced alone until his ammunition was gone. After eliminating thirteen of the enemy, he withdrew to secure a rifle, more ammunition and medical treatment. Seeing a soldier within the area, he grabbed a nearby rifle and eliminated him. Minutes later he saw an enemy nest and returned their fire until the remaining Germans surrendered.

First Lieutenant Beryl R. Newman, U.S. Army
Company F, 2d Battalion, 133d Infantry, 34th Infantry Division
May 26, 1944
Near Cisterna, Italy

The Men Who Were My Life

My men were my life. They liked to have me lead them. I told them when I ordered them "down," before I got done speaking, I wanted them on the ground—and this saved lots of lives. I was in charge of the company while training in Ireland, and I taught them nonstop for twenty-six weeks in the hills. We trained while the others platoons were on guard duty. We were in the 2d Battalion, Company G.

My men thought so much of me that they bought me a new dress uniform, made in London, England, and a dress coat. The best was none too good, they said; they knew I had a wife and three children at home, and I was low on money as a second lieutenant.

In Ireland our officers rode trucks to protect goods and materials. Since they liked that better than training, they put off the training on me. In England we guarded the British headquarters because they had problems with saboteurs. The commanding officer told us no one would be allowed out of the gates. I gave the guards the order and told them no one, absolutely no one, went out after twelve o'clock.

One night officers came by and said they were going out. My men said no to them. They started through the gates and a guard fired through the car door and shot an officer in the leg. I thought I was in for trouble, but I never heard a thing about it.

My soldiers were excellent, and I loved them as much as they loved me.

Captain B. R. Newman

Photo taken at Michigan's Own, Inc., Military and Space Museum, Frankenmuth, Michigan.

... caught in heavy rifle and machine-gun fire that had wounded a corpsman and two of eight stretcher bearers carrying two wounded marines, Pierce took charge and rendered first aid while exposing himself, drawing the enemy's fire and attacking with his weapon and risking his own life to save his patients. After eliminating one enemy, he lifted a wounded comrade to his back and ran unarmed through deadly fire across two hundred feet of open terrain. Despite exhaustion, being weaponless and against warnings, he ... traversed the same hazardous path and went back to rescue the lone remaining marine.

Medical Corpsman Francis J. Pierce, U.S. Navy
2d Battalion, 24th Marines, 4th Marine Division
March 15–16, 1945
Iwo Jima, Volcano Islands

The Common Bonds

There are so many stories that Francis told us it's hard to focus on just one. I wish someone had asked these questions before some of our heroes took their valuable life experiences with them.

Francis J. Pierce was the father of four, two sons by his deceased first wife, Lorraine, and we had two girls. He was a good man and a good father. His headstone simply reads as he wished: "He Served His Country."

After the military, in 1946, he left his hometown of Earlville, Iowa, and joined the Grand Rapids Police Department in Michigan, as a rookie patrolman. Along the way, he was promoted to Accident Investigator, Motorcycle Patrolman, Captain in charge of the vice squad, Uniform Division Commander and finally Deputy Chief in 1972. He decorated his office with hand grenades, mortar shells and other military memorabilia and was the city's Bomb Disposal Expert. In his spare time, he was a steeplejack and avid hunter. Over the years, he demonstrated the same moxie as a police officer as he did as a soldier. Some of his exploits, in fact, are legendary around the police department.

Frank always stated that each man in his unit was a hero. Each soldier shares some common bonds: a desire to help one's friends, a deep sense of responsibility and an ability to answer to a situation above and beyond the call of duty. Further, he always felt he was holding the Medal in trust for a lot of people. When they honored him, they honored hundreds of thousands of men who could have gotten it, but didn't.

A fitting closing, then, is this last page of a speech Frank gave in 1981:

Our country today reminds me of a story. Some scientists took a frog and dropped it in hot water. The frog hopped out: fast! They dropped him in a second time. Same result. Then they dropped him in a vat of cold water, and he relaxed. What the frog didn't know was that the vat of cold water had a fire beneath it. While the frog relaxed, the water heated ever so gradually. The frog sat there, and the temperature of the water rose slowly, and before long, the frog had been boiled to death.

Isn't that a parable all of us need to hear? We don't know how it is in the frog's world, but in our world, it fits us to a "T."

We are all aware of the theologies and ways of life that are in direct opposition to the word of God. We know the consequences of those actions and would jump straight out of the "hot water" right away.

The danger comes when we begin accepting theologies and actions that will subtly and slowly lead us into those traps of "hot water" that kill.

Madelyn Pierce-Mellema,
remembering her late husband,
Frank Pierce

Aligned in assault positions, across a large area of dangerous open rice paddies, Livingston and his company launched a battle on the village of Dai Do that had been seized by Vietcong soldiers the night before. They drove out the enemy and relieved a stranded marine unit. Although painfully wounded, Livingston courageously led another group of marines and halted an enemy counterattack on nearby Dinh To.

Captain James E. Livingston, U.S. Marine Corps
Company E, 2d Battalion, 4th Marines,
9th Marine Amphibious Brigade
May 2, 1968
Dai Do, Quang Tri Province, Vietnam

Life

Life is what you make out of it.

Life is what you want to make out of it.

Life can be a masquerade.

Life can be a manifestation
of your personal accomplishments.

No excuses, life is fun.

Remember, you and no one else
provide the road map to life.

Jim Livingston

… while his battalion was immobilized by heavy fire and a minefield, Mabry alone advanced, establishing a safe route. Still moving ahead, he assisted his scouts in disconnecting other explosives and capturing three enemies. Racing up a slope against three bunkers supported by automatic weapons, he rushed the enemy with bayonets and rifle fire, and then, as his scouts came to his aid, continued to lead an advance across three hundred yards of fire-swept terrain to fortify their position.

**Lieutenant Colonel George L. Mabry, Jr., U.S. Army
2d Battalion, 8th Infantry, 4th Infantry Division
November 20, 1944
Hurtgen Forest, near Schevenhutte, Germany**

A Man of Action

As a young boy, George Mabry ran into his inflamed home and came out carrying his retarded younger brother.

As though he had stepped on a lighted cigarette, and without saying a word, he left the chair he was sitting in at a pool side to dash four hundred yards to a playground where a seven-year-old girl was laying beside the seesaw she had been playing on. He quickly began administering first aid to her broken arm.

An airline stewardess was deeply cut and knocked unconscious; promptly he administered first aid. Later when asked by the pilot, "How serious is her injury, Doctor?" His reply was, "I don't know, but I recommend she see a doctor as soon as we land!"

He was a man of action: He never waited to see what others would do. He acted.

His favorite quote was, "Do not ask anyone to do anything you would not willingly do yourself"—and that included picking up trash and getting your hands dirty.

George L. Mabry III,
writing of
George L. Mabry

The corporal raced across an open rice paddy field, attacking Vietcong single-handedly with his rifle and grenades, eliminating eight enemies. O'Malley then led his squad into another enemy area, helping evacuate wounded Marines and regrouping the remnants of his unit to join in more fighting. Although seriously wounded three times, he refused evacuation for himself but covered his squad's boarding of the helicopters leading them to safety.

Corporal Robert E. O'Malley, U.S. Marine Corps
Company I, 3d Battalion, 3d Marine Regiment,
3d Marine Division
August 18, 1965
Near An Cu'ong 2, Vietnam

"Always Be Honest and Honorable"

My mother and father emigrated from Ireland. They met, married and became U.S. citizens in New York City.

My three brothers, my sister and I were raised in what now might be considered an old-fashioned way. We were all expected to freely help our neighbors ... shovel snow, carry groceries, run errands ... whatever was needed. We were also expected to have jobs, either before or after school. Once we reached the age of twelve, we contributed financially to our household.

In our Irish neighborhood, joining the armed services seemed to be the thing to do after reaching eighteen. In fact, my childhood classmate and neighborhood friend, Thomas Noonan, Jr., would later also receive the Medal of Honor ... but posthumously.

My brothers and I all joined the Marine Corps at different times.

My father's most frequent admonition to my brothers, my sister and me, while we were growing up, was "Always be honest and honorable."

I've tried to do that. They are good words to live by.

Bob O'Malley

... caught in a late-night attack, Merli disregarded the wrath of enemy fire, maintained his position, covered the withdrawal of American riflemen and broke the force of enemy pressure. With one man killed and eight surrendered, Merli played dead until the enemy withdrew. Staying at his weapon, he fought alone throughout the night and by daybreak, left nineteen Germans dead in front of his position.

Private First Class Gino J. Merli, U.S. Army
Company H, 2d Battalion, 18th Infantry, 1st Infantry Division
September 4–5, 1944
Near Sars la Bruyere, Belgium

Of Preparedness and of Families

Medal of Honor! Hero! It is really hard for me to believe.

I was born in Scranton, Pennsylvania, one of five children. My three brothers and only sister all served in the military. You have heard of the "runt" of the litter?— well, that was me. I'm not tall like John Wayne, nor as handsome as Robert Redford, but this runt really puts up a good front and really puts up a good fight.

You understand, it wouldn't be fisticuffs. With me, it had to be brain over brawn. When you're of slight build, you have to out-think your opponent, you have to have a ready response to any occurrence. Be ready to meet any emergency. Sort of like a good Boy Scout—be prepared! This attitude helped me through my youth and certainly came to my rescue in World War II. It serves me well in civilian life.

People are always faced with decisions to make, and when you are married and have children—especially today—this attitude of preparedness comes in handy. My wife and I have had our problems, just as all families do.

My experiences with (sort of) having to fight my way up to adulthood and through the "Big One" of World War II, and from mingling with all people, overseas and in our country, have pointed to an additional insight. This insight has been driven home to me through all types of conflicts—financial, color, race, creed—to mention only a few. It has helped us raise our children with a proper outlook on life: Desire to help all people.

From that desire, my wife and I have tried and still try to live to set a good example to our family, to our neighbors, to our friends and to our community as a whole.

When I returned to Sars la Bruyere, Belgium, in 1995, I prepared a short statement that I gave to the gathered citizens through an interpreter. I think it expresses in short much of my wartime experience:

> *I do not think anyone knows what it is like to be plucked from a loving family ... warmth, comforts, etc. ... except the men who became my family in a war-torn foreign country.*
>
> *You do not know the language. You do not know the people—but you understand the situation.*
>
> *Guns are firing, cannons are booming, bombs are bursting. Men are screaming— death is the only scent in the air and cries are everywhere!*
>
> *You are no longer a person ... you are a killing machine. ... You think, "My new family, and the men I came with are dying ... help them ... get rid of the ones that are killing them.*
>
> *Make this stop—make this stop!!!!*

Live to serve, and you will live a rich full life!

Gino Merli

... commanding a plane rescuing air force personnel shot down in the Bismarck Sea, Gordon flew boldly into the area, making three landings in full view of the Japanese to rescue the nine men. Dangerously overloaded, he miraculously took off, only to receive a report of more Americans stranded in a rubber life raft close to enemy shore. He promptly turned back, set his plane down amidst heavy fire from Kavieng Harbor, took aboard the six survivors from the raft and again amazingly ascended, heading toward friendly land.

Lieutenant Nathan G. Gordon, U.S. Navy
Commander, Catalina Patrol Plane, Patrol Squadron 34
February 15, 1944
Over the Bismarck Sea, Vitu Islands, Southwestern Pacific

Tender Words

My grandfather, Robert E. Lee Bearden,
was a Methodist minister
in the North Arkansas Conference for fifty years.

I enlisted in the Navy V5 pilot program in May of 1941,
and shortly before I was to report,
he reassured me:

"Nathan, it isn't so bad to die fighting for the country you love."

I remembered those words
during several crucial experiences in World War II.

Nathan Gordon

With only a river separating his fire support base from a battalion-size Vietcong group, Davis provided covering fire for his men until an enemy blast threw him into a foxhole. He returned to a burning howitzer to aim and fire it; although injured several times, he continued reloading and firing. Then, barely able to swim across a deep river, Davis crossed it to rescue three Americans.

Private First Class Sammy L. Davis, U.S. Army
Battery C, 2d Battalion, 4th Artillery, 9th Infantry Division
November 18, 1967
Near Cai Lay, Vietnam

Where the Credit Belongs

We find this in our study of social development the human creeds: First, might makes right; second, knowledge is power; third, goodness is greatness.

Humanity has outgrown its first creed, is distrusting the second and is apprehending the third.

Under the first, monarchy was the form of government. Under the second, aristocracy.

Under the third, democracy will appear. Under the first, the warrior was king; under the second, the philosopher and under the third, the servant will be master.

In the light of eternity past, I read that a humanity's greatness was measured by the ability to make the world serve it, but in the light of eternity to come, people's greatness will be measured by their ability to serve humanity.

Under the monarchy, there were slaves. Under the aristocracy, there were wage earners. Under democracy all will be fellow workers. You may call this a utopian dream, but it is the logic of events. It is not the critic who usually does the deeds of humanity, not the man who points out how the strong man stumbled or when the doer of deeds could have done better.

The credit belongs to the man who is actually in the arena; whose face is marred by dust and sweat and blood; who strives valiantly; who errs and comes short again and again; who knows the great inhumanism, the great devotions and spends their self in a worthy cause; who at the best knows in the end the triumph of high achievement; and at the worst, if failed, at least fails while daring greatly so that his place shall never be with those cold and timid who would know neither duty, honor nor country.

Sammy L. Davis

… while commanding a "Green Beret" Special Forces camp during a violent battle lasting five hours with heavy casualties on both sides, and despite severe wounds to his face and body, Donlon dashed through gunfire and grenades to keep the enemy from overrunning his unit. He moved from position to position, directing fire until the enemy retreated and then administered first aid to the wounded.

Captain Roger Hugh C. Donlon, U.S. Army
Detachment A-726, 7th Special Forces Group, 1st Special Forces
July 6, 1964
Near Nam Dong, Vietnam

A Mother's Blessing, a Wife's Prayer

The first words of prayer that I recall learning came from the voice of my mother as she awakened me in the morning or tucked me in at night … . Gently making the sign of the cross on my forehead, she said,

"Good morning, sweet Jesus, good morning, sweet Mary, I give you my heart and my soul; keep me from sin this day and forever."

Even today they remain my first and last conscious words of each day.

I never met another woman with the same deep, pure love and faith in God … that is, until I met Norma. When we married, my Norma selected a very wide and striking gold wedding ring for me. Upon it she had her favorite prayer inscribed: *"What we are is God's gift to us. … What we become is our gift to God."*

The love, faith and devotion of these two women have always been my inspiration and continues to be my strength.

Roger H.C. Donlon

… after three days of fighting near Brest, Hallman advanced alone, leaped into the focus of German defenses, fired his carbine, hurled grenades and ordered those enemies not dead to surrender. Eventually, seventy-five more Germans in the vicinity surrendered, allowing the Americans to advance and capture Fort Keranroux.

Staff Sergeant Sherwood H. Hallman, U.S. Army
Company F, 175th Infantry, 29th Infantry Division
September 13, 1944
Brittany, France

The Man Within the Child

In my heart are many stories I frequently bring to mind about Sherwood. As I write, I think back to a time when I was the young wife of a then prosperous retailer who conducted his business from a specifically built refrigerated van to contain the wares of a small supermarket. The year was 1942.

The business grew to the extent that he could no longer accommodate all of his customers. We agreed that I would take care of a selected group of clients and call them on Thursdays to take their weekly orders and fill them the following Saturday mornings with the help of a teenage student.

So it was that on a Thursday, Annie, one of my customers, unfolded this story of Sherwood. She was a farm lady, approaching her senior years, and the mother of several children. Her son Tom was the same age as Sherwood, and they had become close friends.

Sherwood was born and raised within the borough limits of Spring City, and Annie's family farm was adjacent to the borough. It was a favorite place for Sherwood and Tom to play. Tom had lost one of his eyes, and Sherwood being the person he was took on the responsibility of looking after him. Tom proved to be as mischievous as any other boy.

As Annie spoke on, the boys were together in third grade when someone threw a "spitball" that hit the teacher. No one would confess to being the culprit, so the teacher set the punishment: The entire class would lose their recess for the year. Worse still, it was only early fall.

To this the teacher added, "unless Sherwood wants to admit to it." Realizing that Tom had done it, and wanting to cover for him, Sherwood immediately confessed—losing his recesses for the balance of the year. The teacher never was the wiser that she dealt out the penalty to the wrong person.

This incident is one of many in Sherwood's young life when he reached out to help others. It was unthinkable for him to see another in need if he could do something to prevent it.

As an adult, his heart was always full of charity for his fellow man. And of course, among his other outstanding attributes were his pleasantly cheerful demeanor and his strong resolution.

It has frequently occurred to me that he must have felt great pain in destroying the enemy who he would have thought of as his brothers under other circumstances.

This was the man that the world has lost in exchange for a foothold at Brest.

Virginia D. Hallman,
remembering her husband,
Sherwood Hallman

... as a hospital corpsman, Charette moved through a barrage of small-arms and mortar fire, rendering assistance to his fallen comrades. When an enemy grenade landed within a few feet of a marine he was attending, he immediately threw himself upon the wounded man, blocking the entire concussion. Although sustaining painful facial wounds, he selflessly and relentlessly continued to medically aid others in his unit.

**Hospital Corpsman Third Class William R. Charette, U.S. Navy
Company F, 2d Battalion, 7th Marines, 1st Marine Division
March 27, 1953
Panmunjom Corridor, Korea**

Families Are Special

My parents died when I was five years old. My sister and I were raised by an unmarried uncle. His name was Albert Furlong. We are eternally grateful to him because he kept us out of foster homes and kept us together. He tried very hard to make us a family.

We had several housekeepers that helped out from time to time, but the burden of taking the responsibility of two young children must have been overwhelming.

I thank God every day for allowing Lou, my wife, and I to raise our children as a family and now for giving us those wonderful grandchildren.

Bill Charette

After taking over the duties of a fallen comrade, Jacobson promptly destroyed an enemy aircraft gun, two machine guns and a rifle emplacement. He neutralized a pillbox, opened fire on a tank and climaxed with a lone assault against a blockhouse during the marines' battle at Iwo Jima. All told, he destroyed sixteen enemy positions and eliminated nearly seventy-five Japanese.

Private First Class Douglas T. Jacobson, U.S. Marine Corps Reserve
Company L, 3d Battalion, 24th Marines,
4th Marine Division
February 26, 1945
Hill 382, Iwo Jima, Volcano Islands

"Corpsman, Corpsman!"

It was "O dark thirty," Marine Corps slang for very, very early—3 A.M., to be exact. The day was February 19, 1945, the target Iwo Jima. Not many of us had slept. When you're going ashore in the morning, who can sleep? The ship's PA system had awakened us with "Reveille for all hands," followed by "All troops lay down to the mess deck at 0330 for chow."

As usual, the navy went all out for breakfast. They always did on invasion day—steak and eggs, turkey with mashed potatoes, ham. You name it, they had it. Since this was my fourth landing, I chose the old standby—S.O.S., creamed beef on toast. That, I knew, would stay with me.

At 0415 the PA system barked, "Land the landing forces." This was it.

By 0530, the "wave" (first boat wave) that I was in was circling or, as the Marine Corps put it, "cutting holes in the ocean." We were about twelve thousand yards from the beach. Our wave was the first. There were seven amphibious tractor waves in front of us. They were supposed to land starting at 0900. We, who had been through this before, knew that all the waves would be delayed, and we'd be lucky to be ashore by 1000 hours (our scheduled time).

The word came back, "Move up three thousand yards." The waves straightened out and, in a line, we advanced toward the beach. All we could see of the island were the explosions of naval gunfire. It was massive. We reached the nine thousand yard line and started circling again. This moving up a few thousand yards and circling continued for five hours. It was 1100 and, except for the smoke and fire, we could plainly see the island. At 1130 hours, the word was passed to "Move up to the four thousand yard boats" (these were patrol craft that controlled the movement of the waves).

After more circling, at 1200 (lunchtime, but then, who paid much attention to it?) we formed up again and moved to the two thousand yard line. We again began to circle, but the word was passed, "Form up." We did so, and then came the hated words: "Hit the beach."

The two ten-craft LCVP waves headed ashore. The coxswain had the LCVP wide open. We crouched down, hoping we would get ashore in one piece. One marine was in the bow. His job was to tell how close we were to the beach, because when you did hit it, each and everything—and everyone—was thrown forward.

Five hundred yards, three hundred yards—many of the marines prayed, others tried to crouch as low as possible—two hundred yards, one hundred yards, fifty yards, "KA-BLAM!", a projectile of some sort slammed into the ramp. "This is it!"

The boat struck ground and slid toward the beach. The ramp stayed up—everyone yelled at the coxswain, "Drop the ramp, drop the ramp!" He tried, but it was stuck. About five marines stood back and then lurched forward, butting the door with their shoulders, and "crash," the ramp was down, and out we went.

I ran forward off the ramp into ankle-deep water. "Well," I thought, "not bad, considering a couple of times I'd been waist deep"—and then there was the uphill attack onto the terraces behind the beach.

The ground, black sand really, was ankle deep, and it was like running in glue (it was volcanic ash). We got inland about twenty yards and started digging in. One good thing about the sand was that it was easy to shovel.

We couldn't see much because of the smoke. Every few minutes there would be an explosion followed by cries of "Corpsman, Corpsman" (navy medics). More shells were landing and then the word was passed, "Get off the beach." We started up the terraces toward Motoyaman #1, the first airfield. We'd moved forward and upward five or ten yards when suddenly the air was full of "zing," "zing," and an explosion or two—and again those dreaded words, "Corpsman, Corpsman, help!" tingeing

We continued forward and upward, but for every five yards there were more explosions and then what seemed like a thirty-minute wait. The words exchanged seemed almost all the same, typically heated by battle, expletive laden. Someone hollered, cursing: "What the _____ did the first waves do?" Then someone hollered back, "Die, you dumb _____ !"

Then, after a seeming eternity, it was near dark. The sun was about to sink below the horizon. We'd finally reached the airfield. Five hours to advance one thousand yards of supposedly secure ground ... .

We started digging in. We were actually on the very end of the north-south runway. We dug in so that when we looked up, our eyes would be level with the runway. This was a good foxhole position because the terraces fell away behind us down to the beach.

Someone mentioned that it was chow time. The retort came back fast: "Who the _____ is hungry?"

The night started easily enough—one marine on watch, two off sleeping. Then 2400 hours and I was off. I awakened Jonesy and said, "Hey, you're on." He mumbled, "I just got to sleep." I replied, "Too bad, you're on."

Suddenly, to our left and right everything broke loose. "Bonzai, Bonzai!", and the marine answer, "Bang! Bang! Bang!" Then, "Bonzai _____, you son-of-a-_____ !"

The Japanese didn't approach us, as they knew they'd have no cover or concealment, but fifty yards to the right and fifty yards to the left they could. Off the runway, there was cover and concealment, which they used to full advantage. The hollering and gunfire and grenades continued until 0130.

Then all was quiet ... except for, "Corpsman, Corpsman—please God, Corpsman."

Douglas T. Jacobson

For five days and six nights in bitter, subzero weather, Barber and his company defended a three-mile mountain pass against a regimental-size attack by North Koreans along the critically important route from Yudam-ni to Hagaru-ri. Although injured in the leg, he moved up and down the fighting lines, commanding from a stretcher. At the end of the epic stand, only 82 of his 220 men were able to walk away, but they had eliminated more than 1,000 enemy soldiers.

Captain William E. Barber, U.S. Marine Corps
Company F, 2d Battalion, 7th Marines, 1st Marine Division
December 2, 1950
Chosin Reservoir, Korea

Help Along the Way

As I look back on my life and experiences, my memories are drawn to the generous help I've received along the way. That help started within our large, caring family on our eastern Kentucky farm. For my parents and our brothers and sisters, helping one another was a natural, normal part of their way of life.

As one of the younger children, I received more than I gave. I later came to realize that the affection and selfless actions of my family shielded me from the worst effects of the Great Depression. In the midst of the depression, as my parents and I were trying to find a way for me to enter college, my older brothers and sisters provided financial assistance that made college possible. They also helped with advice, example and encouragement that made college study meaningful.

My wife, the former Ione Lea, tops my list of those who have helped me and others. Our marriage in 1942 brought into my life a partner with a special motivation to help those around her—and the ability to be effective at it. Even as she found time to be helpful to many, our children and I always came first. My marine duty assignments required us to move many times. At each new location, she handled the arrangements that resulted in an orderly, loving home for our family. On each of my several overseas assignments, Ione did the work of both of us and kept our children properly cared for, secure and untroubled. Their mother's example and their own values have combined to instill the same helpful spirit in our daughter, Sharon Waldo, and our son, John.

I have received help every step of the way throughout my Marine Corps career. An outstanding example of that help occurred in late November 1950 during combat in the Korean War, when a marine artillery battery delivered fire support that made it possible for the marine rifle company I commanded to hold a vital mountain pass. The supporting artillery battery (How Battery, 11th Marine Regiment) and my company (Fox company, 7th Marine Regiment) were units of the 1st Marine Division.

A meaningful picture of the extent and value of the help extended by How Battery necessarily includes basic information on the operational situation, locations of marine forces involved, terrain and weather.

The 1st Marine Division, twenty thousand in strength with reinforcements, landed at Wonsan, on the east coast of North Korea in late October. The division launched an advance to northward, with the Yalu River (the boundary between North Korea and Manchuria) as its final objective. Near the end of November, the division gained control of the Chosin Reservoir area and the seventy-mile connecting road to the port of Hungnam, a port forty miles north of Wonsan.

In the afternoon of November 27, two of the division's three infantry regiments, eight thousand with attachments, launched an attack to the northwest from the village of Yudam-ni, at the northwest tip of the reservoir. That attack was soon stopped by a numerically superior force (150,000, it was later learned) of the Chinese Communist Army that had suddenly moved from Manchuria and entered the war. Within a few hours, division strong points at the villages of Hagaru-ri, fifteen road miles south of Yudam-ni, and Koto-ri, twelve road miles south of Hagaru-ri, were surrounded by the outnumbering Chinese. The division was ordered to defend in place.

The terrain between Hagaru-ri and Yudam-ni is mountainous, irregular and generally bare of vegetation. The narrow, dirt-surface connecting road reaches its highest point at Toktong Pass, midway between, and approximately three thousand feet higher than, the two villages.

The weather was bitter cold, with nighttime temperatures down to minus 30° Fahrenheit. The extreme cold made even the routine activities difficult, time-consuming and exhausting. Ice-covered vehicles and weapons required special care and attention to operate. The hard frozen ground made digging-in ten times as difficult as normal.

In the afternoon of November 27, Fox Company moved from Hagaru-ri to Toktong Pass and established a perimeter on high ground that overlooked the road. Shortly after midnight the northwest half of our perimeter was attacked by a Chinese regiment. In five hours of close combat, Fox Company fought off the attackers, and they withdrew at daybreak back to the northwest, beyond the ranges of our company weapons. By that time we were almost out of ammunition and it was evident that significant support would be required for Fox Company to hold the pass. Our most urgent needs were for emergency resupply of ammunition, close air support and round-the-clock fire support that could be delivered only by artillery. All those needs were met and Captain Ben Read's How Battery was assigned to provide direct support of Fox Company. That was a most auspicious assignment, not only for Fox Company but the entire 1st Marine Division. Toktong was to provide a vital link-up for the break-out of the division a few days later.

From firing position at Hagaru-ri, five air miles from—and three thousand feet lower than—Toktong, How Battery responded to every request. Day and night, for five days, shells landed right on time and right on target. How Battery fires inflicted heavy casualties on the enemy and blunted numerous attacks that would have other-wise reached right into the Fox Company positions. I do not diminish or minimize the skill and courage of the marines of Fox Company when I acknowledge that we would not have held Toktong without the help of the 140 marines of How Battery and their six howitzers.

Captain Ben Read's How Battery performed far beyond normal standards and reasonable expectations and made it possible for my company to survive and accom-plish a vital mission. Forty-six years later, I still know of no comparable support and help by one military unit to another. For as long as any marine or navy corpsman of Fox Company is alive, the help of How Battery, 11th Marine Regiment will be remembered with admiration and gratitude.

William Barber

... without hesitation, Hagemeister rushed through deadly fire to offer medical aid to two fellow soldiers and discovered more wounded, including the platoon leader. Yet he proceeded to brave the fierce battle. Although hit by an enemy sniper, he continued his rescue mission, seizing a rifle from a fallen comrade and eliminating the attacker plus three other enemies attempting to encircle his area. So afterwards, he silenced a nearby machine gun.

Specialist Fourth Class Charles C. Hagemeister, U.S. Army
Headquarters and Headquarters Company, 1st Battalion, 5th Cavalry,
1st Cavalry Division (Airmobile)
March 20, 1967
Binh Dinh Province, Vietnam

Strong Values Are Transparent

When I dropped out of college, I was aware that the likelihood of being drafted was high. I didn't join because I really did not want to go. The memories shared by family members who served during the Korean Conflict didn't paint a beautiful recruiting poster to draw this young man in.

I didn't try to avoid joining because that would not be right. Family values said a person's responsibility was to serve if called.

Being drafted into the army proved to be an adventure and personally good for me. After the initial two years, I spent another twenty-one years serving my country in uniform.

I was never ashamed of what I did in Vietnam. The people I served with were some of the best this country produced: Not that they will be recorded in history books, or live again in movies, but to me they were the best. We protected each other, we became family.

As I write this, I can affirm that hindsight is 20/20.

I've learned that people must be informed to make good decisions. They must also understand that they have certain responsibilities they must meet before or while they enjoy the rights those responsibilities can gain. Only by having strong personal values can a person be expected to make the right decisions.

We have the responsibility to pass on to the next generation those values, but strong values are transparent—the next generation will see right through those people who do not genuinely possess the values they are trying to pass on.

Chuck Hagemeister

… wearing a white robe made from a mattress cover, Dunham crawled up snowy Hill 616 under heavy fire and jumped in front of an enemy machine gun as a bullet seared a ten-inch gash in his back. Indomitable, with his robe now soaked red with blood, he immobilized the gun crew and continued advancing ahead of his platoon, eliminating many Germans and capturing two.

Technical Sergeant Russell Dunham, U.S. Army
Company I, 30th Infantry, 3d Infantry Division
January 8, 1945
Near Kaysersberg, France

Helping Solve Problems

I like to remember my five years in military service
as a great adventure. Then I took a job with the Veterans Administration.

It was there I found I could be a great help with fellow veterans.

I spent thirty years with veterans and their problems,
including prisoners of wars (POWs) from all wars.

Russell Dunham

… although outnumbered by the enemy and shot through the arm, O'Brien continued to lead an uphill assault, fighting the enemy in savage hand-to-hand combat for almost four hours. When the attack halted, he set up a defense with his remaining forces to prepare for a counterattack, personally checking each position and attending to the wounded.

**Second Lieutenant George H. O'Brien, Jr., U.S. Marine Corps Reserve
Company H, 3d Battalion,
7th Marines, 1st Marine Division
October 27, 1952
The Hook, Korea**

Find Out ... and Don't Forget

I was a problem for my parents and my high school in my sophomore year. I distracted the class.

My mother and father went to a great deal of expense, one they could ill afford, to have me enrolled in military school.

My stay was short.

I was called to the superintendent's office. He informed me that I was suspected of being involved in the damage to the Founder's Statue. He further stated that he had talked with my father and informed him that no action would be taken if I would resign.

Three days later, my father drove the two hundred miles to pick me up for what I thought was my return trip home. We crossed two states and had ample opportunity for long conversations, both light and serious. The meat and substance of most of our talks were to never quit trying, even after failure.

Not once did he mention to me the disappointment I had caused him or my mother.

On the afternoon of the second day of travel, we arrived on the campus of what was to be my new residence. Dad drove up in front of a dormitory. We got out of the car and removed my footlocker from the trunk and placed it on the steps. He got back in the car and started the engine.

I asked him, "What am I to do?"

"It's time for you to find out," he replied, "but don't forget to daily ask your 'Good Lord' for guidance. Nothing is impossible if you put your trust in Him."

With that, he left.

I didn't know then that he had previously arranged my enrollment. I should have known better.

I took his advice to heart, and it has buoyed me throughout my life, both in good times and bad.

Dad informed me years later that he had cried most of the way home, and I in turn told him he had made a man of me, and that I loved him very much. He was some guy.

I was fortunate to have been reared in a loving home with a strong religious background, steeped with a deep, abiding faith in the Almighty. I have been totally blessed all of my life and for that I am grateful to my parents and my God.

George H. O'Brien

DeBlanc was leading five other American fighter planes into a hostile encounter with Japanese Zeros when he picked up a call for help from American dive-bombers under attack. He broke off his engagement, plunged downward into the formation, disrupted the attack and remained at the scene to challenge the enemy planes. On his return to base, he blasted two more Zeros from the sky, which had closed in behind him.

Captain Jefferson J. DeBlanc, U.S. Marine Corps Reserve
Marine Fighting Squadron 112, 1st Marine Air Wing
January 31, 1943
Off Kolombangara Island, Solomon Islands

Blessed with the Cajun Culture

I was fortunate to be reared in the Roman Catholic faith and in a community reflecting the "Cajun Culture" of South Louisiana. The depression years helped me set my values at an early age.

We lived a slow pace here in Louisiana during the 1930s. Since money was scarce, I worked at odd jobs on weekends and was fortunate to work in the sugarcane mills as a bench chemist during the grinding season in the fall. In the spring and summer sessions, I attended college in order to complete my advanced education. Since we speak three foreign languages in Louisiana—English, French and Spanish—I had an advantage that proved beneficial to me in later life. The G.I. Bill of Rights helped me to adjust after World War II and to obtain my B.S., M.S., M.A. and Ph.D. degrees.

Louise, my wife, and I celebrated our 50th anniversary on November 18, 1995. Having been in the teaching profession most of my years, and also working in industry for ten, I still enjoy helping students and people.

Today, at seventy-five, I still teach in the public school system part-time and am the director of the local planetarium. I'm also an active participant in the state senior olympics.

Sempre fi,
Jeff DeBlanc

... at night, deep in enemy territory, Howard and his eighteen-man platoon were attacked by a battalion-size group of Vietcong launching various weapons. He organized the defense and calmly moved from position to position, directing fire. Unable to move his legs because of a grenade blast, Howard continued calling in air strikes. At dawn, he warned away evacuation helicopters until he could assure a more secure landing zone for his remaining twelve men—all alive, though all wounded.

**Staff Sergeant Jimmie E. Howard, U.S. Marine Corps
Company C, 1st Reconnaissance Battalion, 1st Marine Division
June 16, 1966
Near Chu Lai, Vietnam**

Sports and Teamwork

Jimmie E. Howard grew up in Burlington, Iowa, and was always playing in some kind of sports. His mother said that the different sport and ball changed with the season.

One of the things he learned from sports was teamwork. He really believed teamwork helped him in his career as a marine.

On "Hill 488" in Vietnam, he was the platoon leader of mostly eighteen and nineteen year olds. Only he and a corpsman were older. He was very proud of his "Indians," as he put it.

After he retired from the marines, he volunteered his time as an assistant coach to the Point Loma High School football team here in San Diego. Jimmie also umpired with little league girls softball.

He loved sports and told me that he loved to be with young people who would become our future leaders.

Our family has wonderful memories—and we miss him terribly.

Theresa M. Howard,
remembering her husband,
Jimmie E. Howard

... after twelve days of unsuccessful assaults at Hen Hill, Craft and five other soldiers advanced until all but he were wounded. Steadily advancing alone, eliminating Japanese along the way, he lifted the pressure so his company could advance. Still in pursuit and facing machine-gun fire, he hurled two cases of grenades and finally threw a satchel charge to seal up the Japanese in a cave where they had taken cover.

Private First Class Clarence B. Craft, U.S. Army
Company G, 382d Infantry, 96th Infantry Division
May 31, 1945
Hen Hill, Okinawa, Ryukyu Islands

Lest We Forget

I spend most of my free time volunteering at the Veterans Administration
Hospital here in Fayetteville, Arkansas.

I've done volunteer work here for the last fifteen years.
Guess I enjoy being around veterans.
We owe so much to our service men and women
that served our great nation.
Seems only right to help them!

Clarence B. Craft

... when his platoon leader was wounded, Crews, along with two others, rushed the enemy amidst machine-gun fire. With both of his comrades shot, he continued to overtake first one dug-in position, then another, and although badly wounded, silenced still another position, causing the remaining enemy to either surrender or flee.

Staff Sergeant John R. Crews, U.S. Army
Company F, 253d Infantry, 63d Infantry Division
April 8, 1945
Near Lobenbacherhof, Germany

The Truth and the Irony

The narrative of my citation of which you are about to read doesn't include the stated day's object for my unit, Company F. It was "To Capture an Aircraft Factory." At the time the factory was guarded by the famous Nazi SS Guards, who were known to fight to the bitter end.

This factory was located one mile under a mountain. It could be reached by a narrow-gauge railroad over a mile deep into the mountain side. The railway, of course, was used to haul out their secret "Jet Engine" weapon: It was awesome.

I didn't make it to see this remarkable facility captured. I was carried off the battlefield. However, as of August 1994, this southern German factory is being used as a tourist attraction.

John Crews

... running in the lead of his company, Colalillo climbed upon an American tank, manned an exposed machine gun and with bullets flying toward him fired at an enemy position, destroying their machine gun. As his tank forged on, he blasted three more positions and silenced all resistance in his area. When ordered to withdraw, he stayed behind to help a wounded soldier back to American lines.

Private First Class Michael Colalillo, U.S. Army
Company C, 398th Infantry, 100th Infantry Division
April 7, 1945
Near Untergriesheim, Germany

Seeing Me Home

When the war broke out in 1941, I was sixteen years old.
I thought this war would be over
before I reached eighteen.
Needless to say, it lasted four years
and I was in the middle of it.
The good Lord saw me home safely,
to whom I am ever thankful.

Mike Colalillo

Waging a lone battle when all members of his fire team became casualties, Cafferata maneuvered up and down enemy lines, killing, wounding and forcing the enemy to withdraw, while waiting for reinforcements. Later that morning, when a grenade landed near fellow wounded marines, he grabbed it and hurled it, but not before he severed his finger and wounded his right hand and arm.

**Private Hector A. Cafferata, Jr., U.S. Marine Corps Reserve
Company F, 2d Battalion, 7th Marines, 1st Marine Division
November 28, 1950
Toktong Pass, Korea**

If He Met You, He Remembered

My unit, Fox Company, was ordered to patrol the Hagaru Airfield in Korea, which was then under construction. My buddy, Kenny Benson, and I were fire teammates in a hole around the airfield. We awoke one morning even colder than most (Benson was his grouchy self). He decided that our hole had to be dug deeper and longer because of me. So, he attacked it vigorously with his shovel. I decided there was no sense in both of us getting sweaty, so I grabbed our canteen cups and headed for the command post to get some hot coffee.

I had my rifle slung over my shoulder, and to my left I saw five bodies who would interdict me. Since there was no way to avoid them, we met. I was hailed with, "Hey, Marine." I stopped and turned to meet them; the voice said to me, "Marine, this is Colonel Litzenberg, Regimental Commander 7th Marines." "I'd like to inspect your rifle, Marine," commanded the Colonel. I thought there was some regulation that I didn't have to give him my rifle in the field but, being a private, I wasn't about to debate the order.

The Colonel looked at my rifle and asked for my serial number. I gave it to him, I think it was 11-215. His next question was, "Is there a round in the chamber?" I answered with a "Yes, Sir." Somebody said to me, "Aren't you aware of the order that was issued that there will be no round in the chamber until you are fired upon?" I replied, "Yes, Sir, I'm aware of the order, but if someone shoots at me I'll just snap my safety off and pour lead." He half-smiled and handed me back my rifle.

The Colonel then asked, "Is there anything you boys need out there?" "Sir, we could use some hot food and bread," I answered. His aide was taking notes of our conversation. "Where are you going?" was the Colonel's next question. I told him to the C.P. to get myself and my fire teammate, Ken, some hot coffee. With that he said, "Where's your hole?" I said to the Colonel, "It's right over there, Sir." "Let's go take a look at it," he responded. So we walked over to the hole.

At the edge of the hole was our piece of canvas spread out on the ground. It had several hand grenades on top along with several magazines for the Browning Automatic Rifle which had the bolt cranked back and the magazine in it ready to go. I'm sure the Colonel took this in with one glance.

And there was Kenny, digging away like a groundhog, unaware of our approach. I said, "Kenny, Colonel Litzenberg is here." Kenny answered, "I don't give a f@#*&%." The next thing you know, he's standing at attention, in the hole! The Colonel shook his head and walked away.

Shortly after this encounter, we did get a hot pork dinner and all the fire teams got a loaf of bread to share. And, wouldn't you know, the cook was a friend of mine, Phil Bavaro. I said, "Phil, fill it up." He looked at me and said, "I have to feed 250 men. You can come back later and see if there's any left." What a pal!

Two years later I was ordered to Washington, D.C., to receive the Medal of Honor from President Harry Truman. At the ceremony, Colonel Home Litzenberg, better known to his troops as "Blitzen Litz," was there. After I introduced him to my family, he told my dad all about the aforementioned episode. I often wondered how he could remember one goofy Private among all the others. But, it was as true as we always said, he loved his men, and if he met you, he remembered you.

Hector Cafferata

Peter C. Lemon — 171

… he saw another pilot crash-land on the battle-torn airstrip that lay between the clash of two thousand North Vietnamese soldiers and a U.S. Army special forces camp at the A Shau. Without hesitation he flew his aircraft into direct fire, landed and taxied through a runway littered with battle debris and parts of exploding aircraft to rescue the downed pilot. He then made his escape, lifting off as nineteen bullets from heavy ground fire hit his aircraft.

Major Bernard F. Fisher, U.S. Air Force
First Air Commandos
March 10, 1966
Bien Hoa and Pleiku, Vietnam

Life-Saving Traits

As I returned home from the United States Navy at the close of World War II, I was but a young lad of nineteen, I believe. I had always had a yearning to fly as long as I could remember.

In talking over my future with my father, I remember saying I thought I would like to take my G.I. Bill and learn to fly. Dad counseled me to use the Bill to get an education and flying could come later.

So I attended Boise Junior College and later the University of Utah, where I received a commission in the air force through the ROTC program. I also received a pilot's slot. I spent a year at Marana Air Force Base in Arizona and Williams Air Force Base. This training had a great impact on my life for the next twenty-seven years in the air force and about fourteen thousand hours of flying. Some of the important traits I've tried to cultivate include:

Dependability
Loyalty
Concern and Respect for Others
Teamwork

These traits proved to save my life.

I greatly admire the men and women who wear the "Blue Suit," and I have great love of flying.

Bernard F. Fisher

When a nearby battery gun position was bombed and heavily shelled by the enemy, and all of its crew members were dead or wounded, Calugas voluntarily ran a one thousand yard gauntlet through heavy fire to reach the battle-torn scene. Upon arrival, he quickly organized a volunteer squad, put the gun back into operation and fired it effectively against the enemy—all while his position remained under constant and heavy Japanese artillery fire.

Sergeant Jose Calugas, U.S. Army
Battery B, 88th Field Artillery, Philippine Scouts, 23d Division
January 16, 1942
Culis, Bataan Province, Philippine Islands

When Our Guns Were Silenced

Several years ago my father was left aphasic and paralyzed; currently he can neither talk nor write.

He has always been a very humble man. He did say just after receiving the Medal that

"When the situation confronted me, I did not have any hesitation to fight and give my life for the cause of freedom and my country.

It was not my assigned duty to go to the front line, for I was a cook. But when our guns were silenced, I was determined and ready to give my life for my country.

I feel great being an American; I am proud to be such and I humbly say, thank you and thank you."

Sergeant Jose Calugas,
by his son and legal guardian,
Jose C. Calugas, Jr.

... overlooking a cornfield at Oliveto, Childers, although injured, ordered heavy fire to enable an advance. Two enemy snipers jumped him, and he eliminated them both. Then, moving valiantly from enemy position to enemy position, he expelled their occupants. Lastly, he single-handedly captured a mortar observer.

Second Lieutenant Ernest "Chief" Childers, U.S. Army
Company C, 180th Infantry, 45th Infantry Division
September 22, 1943
Oliveto, Italy

Of Responsibility and Perseverance

Responsibility and perseverance were two lessons that I had to learn early in life.

For the first nine years of my life, my father and mother lived in town during the winter so that my younger brothers and I could go to school, and we moved to the farm every summer.

When I was about ten years old, my father died, leaving my mother, myself and my two brothers. We moved to the farm permanently because my mother had no income; there was no Social Security, life insurance or other benefits in those days, and we had to raise all of our own food.

The only meat that we had to eat was the meat I brought home from hunting. Bullets were expensive, and we didn't have a large supply of them, so I had to make every shot count. Even then, at the age of ten, I realized the great responsibility that I had to assume, being eldest. Also, I realized the importance of never giving up, because if I didn't assume that responsibility and didn't persist, my family would not have meat to eat.

Later, after I had joined the army and was sent to Europe during World War II, I found out just how important these early lessons in life were.

I had to assume command and take on responsibility for the safety of many men's lives, even though I had a broken instep and couldn't walk.

I had to succeed in taking out two German machine-gun nests with the help of my men, or we all would have died.

Even though my childhood was not an easy one, if it had not been for the harsh lessons of responsibility and perseverance, I wouldn't be around to tell this story today.

Ernest Childers

... as his platoon was being evacuated after an intense firefight with Vietcong, Cavaiani voluntarily stayed on the ground, directing helicopter landings throughout the day and into the night. The morning found him seriously wounded but returning enemy fire; with one last effort, he recovered a machine gun and began firing it in a sweeping motion along two ranks of advancing soldiers as the rest of his platoon was able to be evacuated.

Staff Sergeant Jon R. Cavaiani, U.S. Army
Vietnam Training Advisory Group
June 4–5, 1971
Hill 1050, Republic of Vietnam

Words That Work

I remember being a young man and asking my father what he felt had contributed to his success in life. He told me "Honesty, and making the right decisions" were the major factors that helped him through life.

He went on to say that before he made a decision to do something, he asked himself three simple questions:

"Will what I do hurt my family, hurt my friends and lastly hurt myself? If I can answer yes to any of these questions, I don't do them."

As for honesty, he simply said, "Your word is your bond."

I have lived by these words throughout my life and would hope that anyone reading this book might adopt these words and live by them.

They work!

Jon R. Cavaiani

... ordered to aid another American unit in the dense jungle, Foley's company encountered a strong enemy defense as he took the lead with two platoons in the most intense fighting. With his radio operator and machine-gun crew down, he advanced alone, firing the machine gun even though badly wounded. He then evacuated the wounded and led an assault on numerous enemy gun positions in a battle lasting several hours.

Captain Robert F. Foley, U.S. Army
Company A, 2d Battalion, 27th Infantry, 25th Infantry Division
November 5, 1966
Near Quan Dau Tieng, Vietnam

"We Will Always Remember"

Mr. President, members of Congress, the Cabinet, and Department of Defense, distinguished guests, ladies and gentlemen:

It is an honor to welcome you to Arlington National Cemetery—this sacred ground—this final resting place for men and women who made the ultimate sacrifice for our nation.

We come together today at one of the most important national shrines in America. Surrounding us on these hills, overlooking our nation's capitol, are the monuments and gravestones of men and women from the profession of arms who fought and died for our country throughout its proud history.

It is appropriate that we are here today to reflect on their selfless service. From the first Memorial Day observance in 1868, Americans have come together, setting aside differences of race, religion or political interests to honor our fallen veterans and the values for which they fought and died. This amphitheater has become a sacred place from which we express the dignity of purpose inscribed in the arch above. In the words of Abraham Lincoln, *"We here highly resolve that these dead shall not have died in vain."*

Almost every day there are ceremonies here at Arlington involving school children, veterans organizations, foreign dignitaries or private citizens who simply want to lay a wreath as a way of saying "Thank You."

This amphitheater will continue to be the site where we and future generations will revere those who have given their lives for the freedom we enjoy today. This freedom was not secured without great cost.

On these grounds are buried those who perished in every war in which our nation has fought. From the American Revolution and the Civil War to Desert Storm and Bosnia, visitors here can witness the history of American sacrifice for the freedom we so value.

Today, we remember and pay tribute to men and women who upheld the highest traditions of honor and caring for others.

Across the cemetery you will see American flags placed on every grave. That modest recognition and our humble words of homage seem so slight for the enormous sacrifice they have made for us and for those who follow.

But it is our solemn obligation to remember why they died—to secure the blessings of freedom and to guarantee our American way of life.

Today, we say to them—"We Will Always Remember."

Thank you for your presence here today and the great honor you bestow on those who served our nation so well and whose spirit endures.

Robert F. Foley
Arlington National Cemetery
Memorial Day
May 27, 1996

Peter C. Lemon — 181

Despite being in pain and unable to stand from an enemy grenade that had exploded at his feet, Anderson propped himself on a wall and continued to direct howitzer fire upon the closing enemy, while encouraging his men to fight on. When a grenade landed near a fellow artilleryman, Anderson seized it and tried throwing it. The grenade exploded … seriously wounding him again.

Sergeant First Class Webster Anderson, U.S. Army
Battery A, 2d Battalion, 320th Artillery,
101st Airborne Infantry Division (Airmobile)
October 15, 1967
Tam Ky, Vietnam

About Life, from Home

As a young boy I was taught some very good values
about family life and relationships
that I have never forgotten.

I learned to be successful, and to accomplish my goal in life
with honesty, loyalty, patience, self-respect,
respect for others, hard work
and to treat others as I would like to be treated.

I passed these values on to my children.
They are adults now, and I am very proud of them—
as they are of me.

Webster Anderson

... taking over as platoon leader when his lieutenant fell wounded to hostile machine-gun fire, Bacon single-handedly led the assault to wipe out the gun crew who had fired upon them. When another American platoon moved in to help him, their platoon leader was also wounded and Bacon assumed the command to continue leading the combined two platoons in the fight, eventually allowing the rest of the company to move forward and eliminate all other enemy positions.

Staff Sergeant Nicky D. Bacon, U.S. Army
Company B, 4th Battalion, 21st Infantry,
11th Infantry Brigade, Americal Division
August 26, 1968
Near Tam Ky, Vietnam

Knowing the Cost, Expressing the Value

Our Founding Fathers knew that freedom comes with a very expensive price tab. It was going to cost many American lives. They also knew, in July of 1776, when they signed the Declaration of Independence, that they had probably signed their own death warrant.

This is a great country, One nation under God. A nation of prosperity and respect for our people, their liberty and freedom. I believe that our forefathers made a clear, forthright declaration of our dependence on our God and Savior in its closing words. "With firm reliance on the protection of divine providence, we mutually pledge to each other our lives, our fortunes, and our sacred honor."

Fifty-six great men signed that declaration, few survived. Five were captured and tortured to death by the enemy, twelve lost their homes and property, two lost sons in the army, one had a son captured and nine died supporting the war.

Such great men have continued to fight and die for this great country! We are a great nation because we have always had great men and women who believe in the same principles and ideals as our nation's Founding Fathers—men and women who trust in God and who depend upon each other. I have lost many a great friend in battle. Young men, who shall never see a tomorrow. His wife and children shall never again kiss the face of their dead hero. Yes, I know the sadness of war, the many lost lives, the wounded. Yet there would be the greater loss of freedom traded for chains, prosperity for hunger, hope for tears, were it not for these great Americans who have always been willing to pay the supreme sacrifice in protecting our nation from tyrants who would exercise their unjust cruelty over our people.

This is an attitude from the heart. It is more important than the circumstances of life, than education, than skill, than money. It is what makes or breaks a country or a people.

We shall always be a great nation so long as we teach our children that the knowledge and trust as provided by the redeemer of mankind, our Lord Jesus Christ, is of paramount importance. With such teaching it is impossible for us to be anything other than great.

A nation is only great when it is made so by its people. Men and women who work hard every day, cultivating this great and blessed land. Never hungry, but feeding the hungry, opening our nation's arms and heart to the poor of the world.

I love this great land called the United States of America, and in all my travels, I have seen none so great. I'll fight for her and even die for her—for this is my land, secured by God and man. If we ever allow God to be removed from us, we shall fail quickly—for what is a nation without God?

Let us remember all those who have perished for our freedom. Don't let their sacrifice stand for nothing in your life. Tell everyone that they made the supreme sacrifice for a great cause—be proud you are an American, and thank God that you are.

Nick D. Bacon

... wounded in a Japanese attack that killed his two companions, Atkins held his position to repel assaults rather than return to safety for medical treatment. For four hours, Atkins remained in his foxhole. He had fired four hundred rounds and was finally able to withdraw for first aid ... while being treated, he spotted an enemy within American lines, grabbed a nearby rifle and eliminated the threat. Soon after, he saw an entire enemy group moving forward and fired so fiercely that the attackers had to withdraw.

Private First Class Thomas E. Atkins, U.S. Army
Company A, 127th Infantry, 32d Infantry Division
March 10, 1945
Villa Verde Trail, Luzon, Philippine Islands

The Shirt off His Back

I am writing for my Grandpa, Private First Class Thomas E. Atkins.

I would like everyone to know he is a very loving person. After the war, my grandfather married my grandmother, Vivian Atkins, and started a family with a wife and seven kids.

He worked days and nights to support the family. And still today, at seventy-five, Grandfather remains a hard worker—he has his own farm.

There's no way for our family to express our feelings for him; he is very much loved and a very kind and understanding man. As the old saying goes, "He would give you the shirt off his back if it was the only thing he owned." That sums the man Grandfather is.

Angie Edwards,
for her grandfather,
Thomas Atkins

... the sergeant was wounded early in the battle, yet he continued stalking the enemy, carrying only a bazooka. He climbed to the top of a knoll, fully exposed, to shout commands back to his unit. His unit couldn't hear the commands, so he ran back and forth, at great risk, to continue directing tank fire into German wooded positions, all the while wounded, in pain and in full enemy view. He stopped two attempted enemy escapes and helped capture more than five hundred men at the Falaise Picket.

Sergeant John D. Hawk, U.S. Army
Company E, 359th Infantry, 90th Infantry Division
August 20, 1944
Near Chambois, France

Held in Trust

"Short Timer" is the term used for men like myself in World War II, with two years service—six months of basic training, six months of advanced training, six months of combat experience and another six to recover.

All of that was but forgotten until this year. The war didn't get me—but the anniversary nearly did! I guess I had hidden it away.

After the service, I struggled for seven years to qualify to become a teacher. During this time I desperately wanted to get married but didn't think I should until I could support my wife. Finally, after three years, I gave in, when it occurred to me I probably would not make it without her.

I lost her ten years ago and had to start life over. It has been out of control since.

Medal? So what? At the time it really seemed to be an additional burden to bear along with my disabilities. Then, just when I started teaching, our first child, age six, was killed by a car on his way to school. I spent thirty-one years in a local school district as both teacher and principal.

I am being honest in saying that I had some real doubts about the Medal at first. Weird story, my action was, in August 1944, and I received word of the award, with no previous warning, in June of 1945. Why me? For what?

"Winner," "Hero," were the words used. I had many misgivings and rejected those words.

There are no winners in the game of war and to call me a "hero" suggested I had done something more than the people I served with—and that I never could accept. To this day I still talk of "what happened to me," rather than "what I did" with regards to the award.

My overall premise is very simple. I consider the Medal as not a personal thing, not belonging to me. It is a symbol of honorable service in defense of my country! I hold it in trust for all who have served. With this, it becomes easier in my mind to be more specific.

The Medal-Symbol belongs to:

First: Those who gave their lives. There is nothing more you can do.

Second: Those of us who served and hoped we left the world a better place.

Third: Those who serve today to keep what we achieved. Anyone who thinks it could be preserved otherwise is a fool.

I sum up what happened to me with a short sentence, which I'm sure is not original. "I came when I was called, and I did the best I could."

Never do I forget that I was not alone!

"Bud" Hawk

… without orders, on his own initiative as lead scout, when his platoon was pinned down by intense enemy fire, Crawford crested a hill and single-handedly destroyed three machine gun emplacements. He was captured by the Germans and later released, but the army, presuming he was dead, presented the Medal of Honor posthumously to his father.

Private William J. Crawford, U.S. Army
Company I, 142d Infantry, 36th Infantry Division
September 13, 1943
Near Altavilla, Italy

Fifty Years Ago

Fifty years ago, May 1945, World War II ended in Europe when Germany surrendered to the Allies.

I was on the first ship to depart from Le Havre, France, in May. It was the happiest day of my life when that ship pulled into New York harbor and the "Lady in the Harbor" came into view. Everyone on that ship rushed to the side to view that great statue and let out a deafening shout of joy that could be heard for miles. I said to myself "never again will I leave these shores." Fifty years ago next month, my wife Eileen and I were wed in Colorado Springs, Colorado, and will be celebrating our anniversary soon. Fifty years ago this coming March, we moved into our present home. Our two children grew up there—as well as many pets. We were fortunate to find this small-acreage home in the foothills north of the Air Force Academy. As I write, this being the month of Thanksgiving, I'm thankful I survived throughout all those fifty year events and still am enjoying life.

Below is a poem that I first read in a USO Club over fifty years ago in Oran, Algeria, in April 1943. It was good advice then, and it's good advice today:

Be the Best of Whatever You Are

If you can't be a pine on the top of the hill,
Be a scrub in the valley—but be
The best little scrub by the side of the hill;

Be a bush if you can't be a tree.
If you can't be a bush, be a bit of the grass,
And some highway some happier make;

If you can't be a muskie, then just be a bass—
But the liveliest bass in the lake!

We can't all be captains, we've got to be crew.
There's something for all of us here.
There's big work to do and there's lesser to do
And the task we must do is the near.

If you can't be a highway, then just be a trail.
If you can't be the sun, be a star;
It isn't by size that you win or you fail—
Be the best of whatever you are!

William J. Crawford

Vastly outnumbered during an intense enemy attack, Lemon and eleven other members of two squads responded with small-arms fire and grenades. Lemon openly moved from position to position, repulsing the charging adversaries. Realizing their post was perilously close to being overrun, he grabbed a machine gun, stood fully exposed atop an embankment and fired on the enemy. Although wounded numerous times, Lemon refused to be evacuated until the enemy had retreated and all his injured comrades were airlifted to safety.

Specialist Fourth Class Peter C. Lemon, U.S. Army
Company E, 2d Battalion, 8th Cavalry, 1st Cavalry Division
April 1, 1970
Fire Support Base Illingsworth, Tay Ninh Province, Vietnam

The "Whisper"

It's Ironic.
Children are born with the spirit.
We begin to refocus them on the external,
becoming relentlessly driven to find themselves,
when they already knew.

If we, as adults, can quiet ourselves long enough,
we too can hear the "whisper" …
of God's unconditional love.

Pete Lemon

... as commander of the USS Tang *on its final war patrol, O'Kane stood amidst Japanese bullets and shells to launch hits on three tankers, swung his vessel to fire at a freighter and swiftly got out of the path of an onrushing enemy transport. The next day, with ships bearing down from all sides, O'Kane charged the enemy at high speed, exploding a tanker, smashing a transport and blasting a destroyer, all before his own ship went down.*

Commander Richard H. O'Kane, U.S. Navy
USS *Tang*
October 23–24, 1944
Near Formosa Straits, Philippine Islands

Fidelity with Friends ... and Foes

I could write paragraphs about the wonderful man I was married to for fifty-seven years! But I've decided the following quote from a letter written by one of his comrades to me best conveys one of the many admirable qualities of my late husband's character:

... all through my submarine career your husband was a hero and an example for me—a military man toward whom I tried to pattern my own profession. I knew of his courage and tactical gifts and especially his decency. I have told O'Kane stories many times with admiration, but the most poignant to me was his valorous assistance to James Sasaki.

I have done my best to instill in my five sons, all of whom are submarine officers, the ideals he exemplified. I hope that you and your family find great solace in knowing that he inspired and influenced countless numbers of us with his achievements and with his virtue ...

Sincerely,
Ronald Reimann

In the early summer of 1946, after the end of World War II, my husband was ordered to go to Japan to testify in the War Crimes Trials. Still recovering from Beri Beri, and trying to regain the ninety pounds he had lost as a prisoner of war, it was the very last thing he wanted to do. But instead of requesting to be excused from such a distasteful ordeal, he went because he wished to testify for one man by the name of Sasaki who had sneaked a little food to some of the allied prisoners, perhaps at the risk of his own life.

When the U.S. judges heard my husband's stand for Sasaki, they were incensed and told him he could not visit Sasaki in prison. My husband disobeyed—and did visit Sasaki and told him of the support he would get.

After my husband returned to the states, he followed the judgments being made in Japan. When Sasaki was sentenced to twenty-five years, my husband was outraged and would not let it stand. He went to work, obtained the names and addresses of every allied prisoner who had known Mr. Sasaki and was successful in getting each to write his opinions of this one humane Japanese captor.

As a result, Sasaki's term in prison was reduced to seven years.

My husband had to use his own method of getting the court to reconsider. His only regret was that he couldn't get a full pardon for Sasaki.

Mrs. Ernestine O'Kane,
remembering her husband,
Admiral Richard H. O'Kane

… while serving as a sniper team member, Shughart unhesitatingly volunteered along with his team leader to be dropped in to protect four critically wounded comrades at a helicopter crash site surrounded by the enemy. Their request was denied three times because of the risk, but finally they got the go-ahead. With only their sniper rifle and pistol, the two fought their way through intense small-arms fire to the crewmembers and established cover for the injured. Shughart and his team leader continued fighting to save the crew until the enemy so tightened its circle that both were fatally wounded. His actions saved the pilot's life.

Sergeant First Class Randall D. Shughart, U.S. Army
Task Force Ranger, Special Operations Command
October 3, 1993
Mogadishu, Somalia

For Beauty, Keep Climbing

On one of Randy's many trips to western Montana, he and I climbed a mountain called Trapper Peak. This mountain is the tallest in the Bitterroot Mountain Range at 10,157 feet. The summit can be reached, however, with a six-mile uphill hike.

During the journey up the mountain, Randy and I experienced everything between sunny blue skies to blowing snow. This did not slow us down, however, and the attack on the summit continued.

As the air thinned, the need for rest stops increased. During these stops, Randy took pictures of the Bitterroot Valley and the Selway Wilderness.

At the snow line, we took a rest stop to take in the pure beauty of it all. From there we could see the summit, and as we continued, the pace quickened.

With only a hundred yards to go, a strong gust of wind came from the south and blew Randy's brand new Stetson hat off his head. Randy went after the hat as it danced in the strong current off the mountaintop. His efforts were in vain, however, because the hat had disappeared somewhere hundreds of feet below.

With no hope of recovering the hat, we again started for the summit. Randy now used a tan knit cap instead of the Stetson to keep his head warm as we pushed on. Around midday, we reached the summit of the mountain. From the top of the mountain, one could look to the west into Idaho, then north, east and south into Montana. We signed our names to the paper in the jar at the summit and took more pictures.

I wouldn't really understand the significance of the trip until Randy's death some years later.

You see, this climb of Trapper Peak reflects our lives. As you climb through life, you may lose something or someone, but you must keep climbing and enjoy the scenery.

That's how Randy lived his life and how he would want us to continue on without him.

Douglas G. Mason,
remembering his friend,
Randall David Shughart

... during a night rescue operation to save his company commander, Sprayberry's unit came under attack for eight hours. During the battle, he moved his men to protective cover, then crawled out alone to numerous enemy positions and attacked them with grenades and his pistol. He rescued the isolated men and evacuated the wounded, saving the lives of many soldiers.

First Lieutenant James M. Sprayberry, U.S. Army
Company D, 5th Battalion, 7th Cavalry, 1st Cavalry Division
April 25, 1968
Republic of Vietnam

Blue

I knows a little heroman
Maybe he ain't no he-man
Goes by the same shoes
Not so like me, and you's

Yet, he is, yes he is
Sometimes says he is
Ain't no blue albatross
How much you say it cost

Mind if'n I holds it
Sure, don't looks it
What this like inside
Real heromen, all died

Must be hiding something
Sees a mark, gets jumping
Well did once, do again
You done it for a friend

The hoop son, another time
Fool em again, every time
Gives em a true measure
Tells em, been a pleasure

What's his alone, to give
What's he got to live
Gives em what they after
Else they plays it faster

I knows a little heroman
No, ain't a real he-man
I knows a little heroman
Guess, he's just hu-man

J. Sprayberry

Appendix

Congressional Medal of Honor Recipients, 1863–2000

Action	Army	Navy	Marine Corps	Air Force	Coast Guard	Total
Civil War	1,195	308	17	0	0	1,520
Interim 1865–1870	0	13	0	0	0	13
Indian Campaigns	424	0	0	0	0	424
Korean Campaign (1871)	0	8	7	0	0	15
Interim 1871–1898	0	98	2	0	0	100
Spanish-American War	30	64	15	0	0	109
Samoa Campaign	0	1	3	0	0	4
Philippine Insurrection	69	5	6	0	0	80
China Relief Expedition	4	22	33	0	0	59
Interim 1899–1910	0	48	2	0	0	50
Philippines (1911)	1	5	0	0	0	6
Mexican Campaign	1	46	9	0	0	56
Haitian Campaign (1915)	0	0	6	0	0	6
Interim 1915–1916	0	8	0	0	0	8
Dominican Campaign	0	0	3	0	0	3
World War I	90	21	8	0	0	119
Haitian Campaign 1919–1920	0	0	2	0	0	2
Second Nicaraguan Campaign	0	0	2	0	0	2
Interim 1919–1940	2	15	1	0	0	18
World War II	323	57	82	0	1	463
Korean War	78	7	42	4	0	131
Vietnam War and Era	156	16	57	12	0	241
Somalia	2	0	0	0	0	2
Unknowns	9	0	0	0	0	9
Totals	**2,384**	**742**	**297**	**16**	**1**	**3,440***

Source: *Medal of Honor Recipients* (George Lang, Facts on File, 1995)
*Seven recipients were awarded medals in two different actions.

Bibliography

Above and Beyond: A History of the Medal of Honor from the Civil War to Vietnam. Boston: Boston Publishing, 1985.

Lang, George, Raymond L. Collins, and Gerald F. White. *Medal of Honor Recipients 1863–1994.* New York: Facts on File, 1995.

United States of America's Congressional Medal of Honor Recipients and Their Official Citations. Columbia Heights, Minn.: Highland House II, 1994.

Congressional Medal of Honor Society

We highly encourage you to contact the Congressional Medal of Honor Society of the United States of America to enhance your understanding of its purpose and services and to gain additional insight into the individuals who are the recipients of our nation's highest award, the Medal of Honor.

Congressional Medal of Honor Society
National Headquarters
40 Patriots Point Road
Mt. Pleasant, SC 29464
Telephone: (803) 884-8862
Fax: (803) 884-1471

About the Author

Peter C. Lemon is one of the youngest living recipients of our nation's highest award, the Congressional Medal of Honor which was presented to him by President Richard M. Nixon for valor in Vietnam. He was also honored by President Jimmy Carter with the Certificate of Outstanding Achievement and is an inductee in the elite Ranger Hall of Fame.

Mr. Lemon is a graduate of Colorado State University. He completed the degree, Master of Science in Business Administration at the University of Northern Colorado and is the 1998 Humanitarian Alumni of the Year.

Mr. Lemon is a national public speaker, entrepreneur, a coach for youth sports, children's advocate and the proud father of three children.

If you would like to contact the author, Peter C. Lemon, he is very accessible by facsimile or in writing.

Peter C. Lemon
Lemco Enterprises, Inc.
P.O. Box 49025
Colorado Springs, CO 80949
Fax: (719) 548-1747